The
OREGON
SHANGHAIERS

Columbia River Crimping from Astoria to Portland

BARNEY BLALOCK

Charleston   London

THE
History
PRESS

Published by The History Press
Charleston, SC 29403
www.historypress.net

Front cover, bottom: *Off Cape Horn,* J. Latham & Co. 1877. *Library of Congress, LC-DIG-pga-01987. Inset*: "A Quintet of Boarding Masters," *San Francisco Call,* May 5, 1899. *Top*: Postcard from author's collection.
Back cover, bottom: "Two unidentified sailors." *Airspy Collection, State Library of Victoria, H2012.59/90. Top*: "Garthsnaid Fore Yard." Glass negative, Allen C. Green Series. *State Library of Victoria, gr004072.*

First published 2014

Manufactured in the United States

ISBN 978.1.62619.430.4

Library of Congress CIP data applied for.

Notice: The information in this book is true and complete to the best of our knowledge. It is offered without guarantee on the part of the author or The History Press. The author and The History Press disclaim all liability in connection with the use of this book.

The Governor doubts Paddy Lynch's guilt for shanghaiing and pardons him, and tells him: "Go thou, and shanghai no more." The penitentiary is no fit place for gentlemen who practice the gentle art of shanghaiing, for none such were ever sent there.
—*editorial comment,* Oregonian, *1906*

For Molly, Mary and John

Crimps and Crimping, wood engraving by David Syme & Co.
State Library of Victoria, picdb127911.

CONTENTS

Introduction

THE GENTLE ART OF SHIPPING SAILORS

From ancient times, vessels that sail upon the oceans have needed ways to assure that there would be sailors to follow the orders of the captain. Oftentimes, slaves were employed in the maritime service—most notably, the galley slaves of the Romans. The British navy used press gangs to go into a neighborhood, where they would capture able-bodied men, enlisting them into His Majesty's service—where to disobey the order of an officer could cause a man to be hanged. The men of these press gangs were called "crimps"—a word derived from the name of a device for trapping fish.

By the nineteenth century, the lot of the merchant sailor had improved to the point where floggings and other inhuman punishments were illegal. However, a sailor aboard a merchant vessel had no more rights than a member of the military for the duration of his contracted voyage. Once a man's name was signed on the "ship's articles," it was against the British maritime law, the laws governing the maritime trade of the United States and the laws of the state of Oregon for him to desert his ship until his contract was fulfilled. Even so, it was estimated that from the time Portland became a seaport until late in the first decade of the twentieth century, about three-fifths of all sailors deserted their ships, either in Astoria or in Portland. This was due to the sailor's boardinghouse and shipping master system transferred to Portland from the older ports, such as San Francisco and New York.

Typically, except during intermittent times when the laws were being enforced, as a vessel came into Astoria (or Portland) after a long sea voyage, it was immediately boarded by a crimp—either a "runner" working for a boardinghouse or the boardinghouse master himself. The crimp, or his runner, would entice the sailors to stay at his boardinghouse "on the tab," almost always promising a better ship with higher pay in the very near future. The sailors would not be paid until they completed their contracted voyage, so desertion meant that they lost their wages to the captain. The strongest impetus to desert was the fact that the men had been at sea for at least three months (usually much longer), were bored nearly to death and had not eaten decent food in many long weeks. In the sailor's boardinghouse, they would be charged exorbitantly for everything from sleeping on a bed of hay to their daily food and drink, as well as any article they may have needed. By the time they were "shipped" by the boardinghouse master, they would owe him several months' advanced wages. The money taken by the crimp was called "blood money." Many is the sailor who went from port to port always in arrears, never having a farthing or a dime to call his own.

In Great Britain, a shipping master was a servant of the Crown. Not only did he assign sailors to ships, but he also saw them paid off, kept books on the wages contracted and paid and oversaw the examination of sailors to see how they should be rated. In the United States, a sailor on a British vessel (the great majority of the vessels were British in those days) was required to sign the ship's articles in the presence of the British consul, vice-consul or his representative. If it was an American ship, he was required to sign in the presence of a United States shipping commissioner, or the collector of customs. The sailors were required to sign the ship's articles of their own free will and to do so while sober. These regulations were to prevent men from being "shanghaied" or to sign while drunk or under the influence of drugs. In the United States, a shipping master was a title conferred on different sorts of men at different times and according to the custom of the port. They may have been men working for a shipping company or for a consortium of crimps, but they functioned as mediators or employment agents. In the case of there being no shipping master, the crimp acted as one himself; therefore the titles "boarding master," "boardinghouse master" and "shipping master" are often used interchangeably in American newspapers. The news editors were also fond of using derogatory terms like "land sharks," "shanghaiers," "blood-suckers," "pirates," "vermin" or "crimps" whenever they felt the material warranted it. All of the crimps referred to their occupation as "shipping sailors." The sailors themselves, however, often referred to these methods as "shanghaiing," as a manner of speaking, even if they willingly signed the ship's articles.

Commercial cargos from Portland were, for the most part, made up of sacked wheat from the Willamette Valley or sacked flour from the local mills and, to a lesser degree, canned salmon and lumber. Until the twentieth century, the vast majority of these cargoes were aboard British vessels, and nearly all cargoes en route to Europe were instructed to go to "Queenstown for Orders"—Queenstown being the port of Cork, in

A sailor being picked to pieces by crimps. *From Watts Phillips,* Wild Tribes of London *(London: Ward and Lock, 1855).*

western Ireland. The harbor at Queenstown saw many hundreds of vessels each year, being the port where the shipping agents would receive the orders for the vessel's final destination by telegraph from London or Liverpool. A cargo could be bought and sold several times while in route, depending on the speculations of capitalists. Until the Panama Canal was finished in 1914, all such shipments needed to go around Cape Horn, a distance of some eighteen thousand miles.

By the end of the 1880s, the ports of Astoria and Portland gained reputations as the worst in the world with regard to violence and dishonesty in dealings with sailors and captains. This reputation continued even after the evil was suppressed, but the crimping itself lasted for about three decades. This book is the true story of the men and women who "shipped sailors." It is drawn from original source material, not from history books. The lack of factual information about these crimps available to the public has given rise to absurd legends, invented by writers of fiction. There would be nothing wrong in this at all, if some of these tall tales were not now purported as historical fact.

This book is not intended to be sensational but is intended as an introduction to some of the neglected characters of Oregon's past. Each person in this

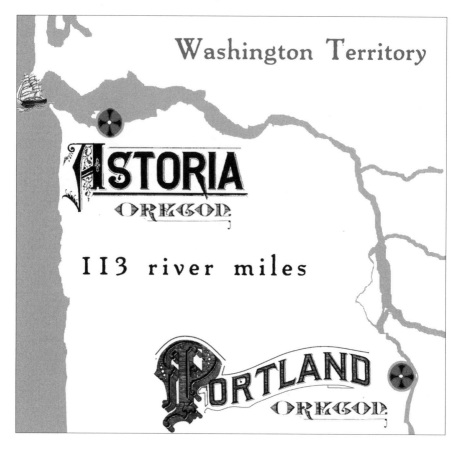

The lower Willamette and Columbia Rivers, Portland to Astoria. *Map by author.*

book is a complexity of influences and passions, in a unique time that will never see its equal. They lived in a day when a mighty civilization was rising up out of the wilderness, and the vanguard of this civilization was a group of unruly souls who secured their place in the new world with either gold coin, law books and politics or with daggers, fists and revolvers. Pity the poor jack-tar who, after four months at sea, comes with hopes of finding hospitality and succor in such a place.

My deep thanks to my brilliant wife, Nektaria, who always makes me look better than I actually am. I am also very grateful to Lisa Penner of the Clatsop County Historical Society for all her help; Peter Grant III for his insight into family details; J.D. Chandler for his sage advice; the helpful staff at the Oregon Historical Society; Aubrie Koenig, Becky LeJeune and Darcy Mahan at The History Press; and Cindy Coffin for allowing me to use her family's materials concerning Carroll Beeby.

CAN ANYTHING GOOD COME FROM SAN FRANCISCO?

GETTING AWAY WITH MURDER

In Portland, it was always whispered behind Jim Turk's back that he had gotten away with murder, which was true, but the story was one that few Portlanders knew. Turk was in the spotlight constantly, but of his past before he took up the trade of "shipping sailors," very little is known. It is certain that he was enlisted in the U.S. Navy during the Mexican War, and in 1847, he participated in the siege of Vera Cruz and the march on Mexico City.[1] Somewhere between then and his appearance in San Francisco, he had a son named Charles, presumably a legitimate son, who didn't live with him. He also acquired a new wife—Catherine—an obese, dark-haired, Irish woman, described as beautiful by some. Beautiful or not, she became a demon when filled with drink—a rampaging, cursing, fiery banshee, well acquainted with police and the misery of drying out in a cell.

In the mid-1860s, San Francisco was still cut off from the East Coast by long treacherous journeys—either by overland mail carriages or by months at sea. It was thus a frontier city, located at what seemed like the ends of the earth. Here Jim and Kate Turk ran sailors' boardinghouses—the first at 811 Battery Street,[2] the second at 114 Jackson.[3] It was their business to supply the maritime trade with fully outfitted, (hopefully) able-bodied seamen to replace the ones who had deserted upon arrival. Records show that the establishments the Turks ran were licensed to sell spirituous liquors to such jolly sailors as sought refuge at their door.

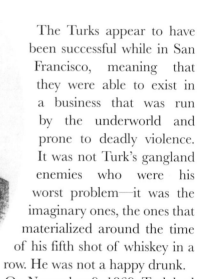

A young James Turk. *Drawing by author.*

The Turks appear to have been successful while in San Francisco, meaning that they were able to exist in a business that was run by the underworld and prone to deadly violence. It was not Turk's gangland enemies who were his worst problem—it was the imaginary ones, the ones that materialized around the time of his fifth shot of whiskey in a row. He was not a happy drunk.

On November 9, 1869, Turk had gone out with a friend, a man named Sullivan, to go racing buggies on the roads outside the city.[4] In the late afternoon, near dusk, they returned, tired and arguing. They put up their buggies and went to Charlie Hanson's Saloon on the corner of Vallejo and Davis Streets. After drinking in the saloon a short while, angry words ensued between the two men, which developed into a fistfight. They were separated by the barkeep, with the help of bystanders, and sent their separate ways.

At six o'clock that evening, after Turk had become staggering drunk, the two men met again in the street outside the New World Saloon on the corner of Vallejo and Front. Turk lunged at Sullivan, and once again the men—by now both of them drunk—were scuffling and punching at each other. One of the owners of the saloon, Alexander Gallagher (called "Dutch Aleck"), stood by laughing at the slapstick antics of the struggling drunks. As the fighting continued, Turk noticed the grin on Dutch Aleck's face and impulsively ran at him, reaching for his knife. In a single, deadly second, Turk plunged the knife—a folding knife, sharp as a razor—into Dutch Aleck's gut. The wounded man, being drunk himself, went back into the saloon, unaware of his injuries. As he stepped into the back room, he suddenly fainted into a pool of blood. Several men rushed to his aid, and

Vallejo Street, San Francisco, looking toward the intersection where Dutch Aleck was murdered. *Lawrence & Houseworth Collection, Library of Congress, LC-USZ62-27414.*

as they lifted him off the floor and on to a table, his intestines could be seen protruding from his abdomen.

An ambulance was called, and Gallagher was taken to St. Mary's Hospital. Police detectives made their way to the scene of the crime to gather evidence—Sullivan himself being the primary witness. They then proceeded to the hospital, where they took down Gallagher's statement, accusing James Turk of being the man who wounded him. The officers proceeded to Turk's boardinghouse, where he was taken into custody and brought to the station house jail. Alexander Gallagher lingered for a day, before breathing his last at three o'clock the following morning.[5]

A postmortem examination showed that Gallagher had died of his wounds, his intestines being severed in four places. Turk was then charged with murder and moved to the city prison. The day following, a coroner's inquest summoned Sullivan to testify, but as Sullivan was too drunk to do so, he was placed in jail to sober up. Several days later, Turk was arraigned and

St. Mary's Hospital, South Beach, where Dutch Aleck died. *Lawrence & Houseworth Collection, Library of Congress, LC-USZ62-27430.*

charged with manslaughter, bail being set at $5,000—a sum that Turk would be hard pressed to raise.

It was thirteen months before his case came to trial, a period of time that the jury must have considered sufficient for the crime. The case was poorly prosecuted, and he was acquitted after the jury had been out a mere ten minutes. Doubtlessly, Turk's defense relied heavily on the fact that Gallagher took so long to realize he had been mortally wounded. Later that afternoon, a reporter for the *Daily Alta California* ran across Turk on the waterfront, blind drunk, shouting, "I'm the chief!" and other self-aggrandizing epithets.[6]

It wasn't long after being released from prison that Jim Turk; his wife, Kate; and baby Frank set sail on a steamer for the Pacific Coast's newest seaport: Portland, Oregon.

PIRATES AMONG PURITANS

From its beginnings in the late 1840s until the period of deep dredging of the Columbia and Willamette Rivers (called "river improvements"[7] by the Army Engineers), the city of Portland was not a normal "wild west" city. Aside from the fact that it was not a city but a mere town by today's standards, it was in no sense "wild." The early travel writer Samuel Bowels wrote in *Our New West*, "The population of Portland is now from eight to ten thousand, who keep Sunday with as much strictness almost as Puritanic New England does, which can be said of no other population this side of the Rocky Mountains at least."[8]

That was just one year before the Turks arrived in Portland and set up their business, the "Sailor's Home," in an area close to the wharves. Portland was newly proud of its designation as a seaport—and one with a new U.S. Customs house,[9] giving it the seal of approval from Uncle Sam as a port that could accept cargo directly from overseas. The vessels that crossed the Columbia bar for Portland were escorted by skilled river pilots under the steam of one of the paddlewheel steam tugs belonging to the Oregon Steam Navigation Co. Deep-sea captains were leery of the river, with its miles-long sandbars, making the passing impossible in seasons of low water. The maritime insurance providers were wary, insisting that any vessel whose hull scraped river bottom be taken to dry dock. Freight was often "lightered" to ships anchored as far downriver as Astoria.

Everyone knew that the Columbia River system, which reached inland for 1,000 miles, needed a major seaport. Astoria, at the river's mouth, was the natural choice, but the town was broke, dependent on the gold rush bankers of Portland and the wealthy merchants, who treated the city as if it were an extension of its own harbor, 113 miles upriver. When the Turks arrived, two of the city's merchant houses, John McCracken and Corbett & Macleay, had successfully sent cargoes directly to Europe from Portland. Portland had known American sailors from coasting vessels since its beginning, but now there were, from time to time, English jack-tars staggering the streets and singing in the saloons. "Jolly Tars," they were called, or the "Jolly Sons of Neptune." They were always jolly, it seems, even when they were being robbed of their life savings and herded like sheep.

It was always Jim Turk's notion that he was a legitimate businessman—even when using illegal means to procure sailors. He knew, and the authorities knew, that the sailor's boardinghouses were an important cog in the machine of maritime business. It was this knowledge that allowed Turk and all the

Early Portland panorama. *Author's collection.*

other crimps—at least the ones who operated outside the shadows—to walk the streets with their heads held high. When sober, Jim Turk presented himself as a man of importance, with oiled hair, clean shaven, smelling of cigars and the finest barbershop lotions. He dressed, or intended to dress, like a gentleman—a gentleman who would wear striped pantaloons with a plaid riding jacket. He was a bully, and thus—like all bullies—something of a buffoon, but his eyes could make another man's blood run cold.

The greater portion of his days were spent in the company of Kate, his Irish love, his royal pain in the ass, his business partner, his worst enemy, his sparring partner and the doting mother of young Frank, to name but a few attributes of this large-boned lady. She was his greatest desire and his greatest shame, for theirs was one of those complex relationships that occur when two people of identical passions and failures marry one another. They loved booze, money, violence and each other—in that order.

It seems an undeniable fact that if Jim Turk looked like the sort of fellow who could murder someone, Kate, when she had been up at the Ivy Green drinking with the other "Irish lasses," was transformed by those alcoholic elixirs into a female entity who looked as though she could slay an entire Persian army.

This first attempt at a sailor's boardinghouse in Portland was a failure, with the business collapsing after about a year. Their try at being the pioneer crimps in the new seaport was premature. In 1873, the Turks returned to San Francisco, and Jim Turk went into partnership with a crimp named MacDonald, opening a boardinghouse on the city front at 23 Vallejo Street,[10] within a stone's toss of where he had killed Dutch Aleck. It was a rough time in the marriage of Jim and Kate. No doubt the "jolly tars" were subjected to some very unjolly scenes between the two. Kate could match—and even exceed—her husband in ferocity and violence, to the point where Jim began to be concerned for the very safety of his toddling little boy.

Things had become so bad that Jim Turk developed a plan of escape. He had been on the lookout for the British schooner *Cultivator*, which was expected in the harbor in late November or early December. The captain of the ship was Jim Turk's brother-in-law from Liverpool. When the *Cultivator* arrived in the harbor, he made a secret arrangement with his brother-in-law to sign on as his steward. This was the lowest job on board, serving as the captain's personal attendant. He would take his son, little eighteen-month-old Frank, to live with his sister in Liverpool. One of the runners from the boardinghouse, a man named James Foy, would ship as an able-bodied sailor. The afternoon that the ship was to sail, Jim Turk, Foy and little Frank went along with the crew as it rowed out to the vessel.[11]

James and Catherine Turk. *Oregon Historical Society, Or Lot 108.*

When Mrs. Turk discovered her son missing, she went into immediate action, descending on the police station like a force of nature. The startled officers at the station were reluctant to become involved, stating to the outraged woman that her husband could not be arrested on a writ of habeas corpus for kidnapping his own son.

Finding no satisfaction, Mrs. Turk then descended on the Harbor Police, men who had no great love for either her or her husband, with an augmented version of her tale in which Turk and Foy were accused of stealing a trunk and other articles belonging to lodgers at the boardinghouse. The Harbor Police then held up the vessel long enough to extract the two men and the child, depositing the men in prison until the situation was sorted out. The incident was reported in the *Daily Alta California* by a reporter who had obtained all of his information from the sobbing mother. According to her, Jim Turk was "a dissipated man, bothersome about the house when drunk, making his wife the object of his ill nature." It wasn't long before the accusations against Turk and Foy were seen to be without merit and the men were set free, but the *Cultivator* was already far out on the bounding waves.

How and where the couple reconciled is unclear, but it wasn't long before they were back together, with business as usual.

During the months the Turks had lived in Portland, they had made themselves known to both the police and readers of newspapers. It seems, however, they were not as notorious for their crimping, blood sucking or shanghaiing of sailors as they were for their actions while under the influence of strong drink—Jim having a tendency toward assault and battery and Kate a penchant for drunken rampages. When an unnamed *Oregonian* writer saw items appearing in the San Francisco news about the Turks' latest escapade, he immediately penned a semi-comic article called, "The Turk Family," whose opening paragraph is worth reading, at least for its entertainment value:

> *The Portland public, and especially the members of the police force of this city, certainly have abundant reason for remembering one Mr. Turk and his angelic and dutiful spouse, Catherine. This detestable pair formerly resided in Portland, and were the proprietors of a low, disreputable sailor's boarding house, near the corner of Front and Ash streets. Turk was a swaggering bully, and never allowed an opportunity to pass by unimproved to display his pugilistic talents, especially when the opponent was physically inferior to himself. His wife was a female*

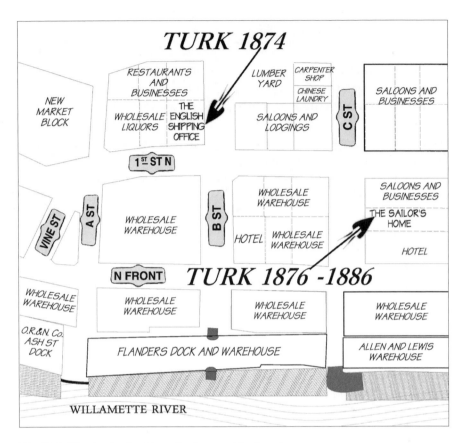

The Turks' Portland sailors' boardinghouses. *Map by author.*

of Amazonian proportions, with a temper alongside which Jezebel was an angel and to which might be added that other commendable trait, intemperance. During her drunken sprees she was a terror to her husband and a source of annoyance to the police. Finally Turk shipped on board an English vessel and left the country.[12]

The story continues on as a reworded version of what was said in the *Daily Alta California*. I wonder, had the author of this *Oregonian* report known that both James and his "Amazonian" wife were headed back to Portland, ready to give the port another try, he may have moderated his sentences somewhat, remembering the beefy fists of the "swaggering bully," Mr. Turk. By early fall of 1874, the Turk family was back in Portland.

THE ENGLISH SHIPPING OFFICE

The Turk family took up where they left off, this time putting some effort into appearing respectable. Jim Turk reported his business to the *Portland Directory* as being the "English Shipping Office, S.E. corner of First and B."[13] It was the first of many respectable names he would try, but the name "Sailor's Home" would, it seems, be reported in the papers no matter what the sign above the door read at the time.

Sometimes Turk would meet the ships at the dock, but usually they would first be anchored in the harbor above Swan Island to wait for a berth at one of the large grain warehouses that lined both sides of the river. Turk would use a dinghy of some sort to go out to the ship. He would climb the Jacob's ladder and put on his charm—he could be charming. He had a pocket full of cigars, which he handed out freely, and he welcomed the boys to Portland, a fine city, with beautiful women, evening entertainments and the finest beer this side of Newcastle. He also stated emphatically that he could do all the boys a big favor and get them better employment on an easier ship, with higher pay. So most of boys deserted, forfeiting their pay to the captain.[14] Turk had them ferried across the Willamette by rowboat to the Sailor's Home, where he took them into his care.[15]

From the moment they came under Turk's roof, each inmate of the Sailor's Home was charged for every necessity and luxury at a rate comparable to, or higher than, other establishments in the city. This might mean normal hotel rates for sleeping on a box full of hay ("donkey's breakfast") and restaurant prices for the infamous sailors' boardinghouse "stews." Of course, the lads were allowed to run up a bill, and of course, they were penniless and had no recourse to this regimen. When the time came that some vessel (which had been loading for weeks) had its last sack of wheat stowed, the captain would buy a crew from Mr. Turk by paying the bills the crew had run up. These bills, which often included rain slickers, boots and other articles of clothing, were provided at "going rates" but were, more often than not, substandard. The money to pay the tab was taken from the sailor's advance wages and usually amounted to several months' pay. It was called "blood money" in the press. Many is the sailor who went penniless from port to port his entire career, for Mr. Turks could be found in nearly every port across the globe.

In those days, with a large number of vessels receiving their final cargo at Astoria, sailors recruited in Portland often needed to travel to Astoria by steamboat to join their ship. It was also to the advantage of Astoria sailors' boardinghouses to have on hand a "boatsman" who could guide a dinghy over the bar so the "runners" could begin to persuade the crew to desert even before the ship was in the harbor.

In 1876, Jim Turk and his son Charles opened a sailors' boardinghouse on Water Street in Astoria. Between Jim, Kate and Charles, they would operate in both ports. The usual arrangement was for little Frank to be as close to his mother as possible, while Charles tried to be in the opposite port from where she was, due to the animosity they felt for each another. The Portland newspapers often referred to Turk as an "Astoria sailor's boardinghouse keeper" even though his Portland boardinghouse was listed in every issue of the *Portland Directory* (except for the year 1889, when he operated solely from Astoria). The dual citizenship was such that Turk even once ran for mayor of Astoria.

BRITISH VICE-CONSUL

Arriving in Portland in 1871, about the same time as the Turk family's first attempt to settle here, was a gentleman merchant named James Laidlaw.[16] He was an Englishman, who would within a few years become Queen Victoria's official representative to the states of Oregon, Washington and Idaho, with the title "British vice-consul." Laidlaw would always remain an Englishman, but he would live in Portland for the remainder of his days, into the second decade of the twentieth century. It was his office that was required by British maritime law to oversee the signing of ship's articles by newly recruited sailors. It is more likely that a clerk of his office took care of these details, but this official duty placed Laidlaw in the uncomfortable position of being subject to the criminal shenanigans of the boarding masters. As such, James Laidlaw became the nemesis of James Turk (and the others), the white knight against the evil gang. Laidlaw, however, was a grownup English schoolboy from an Anglican school at Wanlock-Head, and Turk was a shanghaier from San Francisco with money in the bank and blood on his hands.

Astoria was also equipped with a British vice-consul, an English commission merchant named Peter L. Cherry. It is likely that Cherry signed off on far more sailors than Laidlaw. The crimps were known to be skilled at pulling the wool over Cherry's eyes—a man who was either addlepated or half-blind and deaf to boot. It was his job to see that the sailors were being provided with appropriate clothing and footwear. Rumor had it that the runners, who were signing the name of drunken men sleeping it off in the boardinghouse, would pass the same kit bag of clothing and boots one to another as they entered Peter Cherry's office for inspection.

RACE NOT TO THE SWIFT

The fall of 1877 was dreary for Jim Turk. He had been in several altercations that ended up with him in police court paying large amounts of cash to the city's coffers for problems that were his own and none of the city's business. Kate had her difficulties as well, being the butt of jokes told by prostitutes who had been, at one time or another, taught respect by her fists—respect that was short-lived. Each time one or the other was arrested for drunkenness and brawling, they were treated as if they were some local proverb of excess, subject to open ridicule in the pillory of the pages of the local press.

Late that September, the paper printed a report that read, "The members of the Turk family are again in tribulation. Mrs. Turk was arrested last evening for disorderly conduct and locked up."[17]

A few days before that, a street fight had broken out between a couple runners working for Turk and some runners working for a man named Laugton, who was trying to ship sailors from his hotel, the Howard House, a frame building across from the steamboat landing. A big ex-sailor named Williams jumped into the fray. Turk showed up with his pistol and fired at the man. Williams was certain he had been hit since one of Turk's runners had nicked the back of his neck with a knife. He needn't have worried, since Turk was a poor shot at the best of times, and he was "three sheets to the wind," to use a nautical phrase. The men were so far gone that it took only a single city constable to disarm them and march them through the crowd that had gathered and down to the jailhouse.[18]

After hearing the story from a number of witnesses, as well as the men themselves, the magistrate at police court fined both of them. Turk got the worst of it for firing his gun, but at least it wasn't attempted murder. His fines were twenty dollars for discharging a firearm and fifty dollars for assault and battery. The charge of assault with a deadly weapon was "taken under advisement," which meant that Turk had better behave or that, too, would be thrown at him.

The fines had brought the bank account to a low point. If the deadly weapon charge were to be brought forward, Turk may have had to serve a stint in jail. The city jail was a miserable stink hole from which prisoners were taken to various quarries around the outskirts of the city and forced to turn large boulders into gravel with a heavy sledgehammer. This was no place for a Turk. The anxiety was tense, and the yelling between the Jim and Kate was loud, each blaming the other for the state the family was in. During this period, little Frank either hid in the room he shared with his parents or played in the streets with his urchin friends. It was not a great beginning for him.

Then, on October 12, 1877, it all changed. A well-dressed man with the look of a solicitor arrived from San Francisco on the *Oneida*. He soon found rooms at the Norton House, at the corner of C and First Streets, where he gave his name as T.J. Zingsen and mentioned that he was in Portland to do business with a Mr. James Turk, who had recently lived at 24 Vallejo Street in San Francisco. The innkeeper, and all those whose ears were flapping in that direction, felt a solemn gravity descend upon their thoughts, for if it involved Turk, it probably couldn't be good.

Soon the story that leaked out was that which every man might dream of as a distant fantasy—like becoming president of the United States or finding a genie in an eastern lantern. Mr. Zingsen had given Turk the news that he was now a wealthy man, having been left nearly 30,000 British pounds by his father's brother, who had died in Bristol some years earlier.

Judges and various lesser authorities whose incomes were dependent on a certain amount of graft began a serious reassessment of James Turk as a businessman. Those familiar with their Bibles may have recalled the passage, "I saw under the sun, that the race is not to the swift, nor the battle to the strong, neither yet bread to the wise, nor yet riches to men of understanding, nor yet favor to men of skill; but time and chance happeneth to them all." (Ecclesiastes 9:11)

What came next is a glimpse into the complex nature of James Turk. Whether out of a vacillating sense of thanksgiving to providence or from a deep and abiding cynicism, Turk did the unthinkable and allowed his den to become a house of God.

BETHEL

Since the early years of the nineteenth century, seaman's chapels had been springing up around the globe as a result of the English Evangelical movement and a spreading British empire. This movement was organized by a group calling itself the Seaman's Friend Society and was made up of people—many of them people of means—who were interested in providing help and moral support to the poor sailor. They built seaman's centers, lending libraries and chapels, called "bethels" (House of God).[19]

In Portland, the Seaman's Friend group was made up of men like H.W. Corbett, E. Quackenbush, James Laidlaw and John McCracken, some of the most important men in the state. They were looking to build in Portland a place for the Seamen's Friend Society to use as a center and bethel. It would be a boardinghouse, a library and a shipping office apart from the crimps. Already they had been holding bethel services aboard vessels at the docks, raising the bethel flag to announce the meetings. The national society had recently sent a missionary to Portland, a man named Stubbs, to help make it happen. What happened next is best described in the report written by a nearly speechless reporter.

A very interesting meeting at the Sailors' Home, a boarding house kept by Mr. J. Turk was held in this city last evening. For several weeks past Chaplain Stubbs has been made welcome to the use of the neat and commodious dining hall of this boarding house for sailors on Tuesday evenings. Every arrangement has been made to afford convenience, attraction and comfort to those who attend these services. Several ladies from the city, with Mrs. Stubbs, have lent their influence by singing and other devotional exercises, and with very gratifying results.

Last evening four young seamen signed their pledge of total abstinence, and not less than eight expressed their determination to turn to God and solicited the prayers of Christian people.

Several members of the Taylor street M.E. church were present, also Mr. Cruse and wife, and they will probably enjoy the privilege of leading these sons of the ocean to the churches they represent. These meetings are to continue, we learn, and it would be profitable to the churches to have their representatives present.[20]

COWARDLY PRUDENCE

While continuing to operate from the "Portland House," James Turk went on a buying spree, picking up hotels and restaurants in both Portland and Astoria, including the seventeen-room Grand Central Varieties Saloon in Portland and the Delmonico Restaurant in Astoria.

Jim Turk had never felt the least inclined to share his wealth with Kate, a woman whose dissipation grew more alarming with each passing day. Money did not solve any domestic problems. The irascible Mr. Turk continued to be, as described in the *Alta California* article, a "dissipated man, bothersome about the house when drunk, etc." So much so that in June 1879, Kate once again packed her suitcase and went to live elsewhere. Mr. Turk responded by a notice in the *Oregonian*:

> *NOTICE: Whereas my wife, Mrs. Kate Turk had left my bed and board, without just cause, I caution all persons not to trust her on my account as I will not be responsible for any debts, dues or demands contracted or created by her. James Turk*

Mr. Turk, no longer having a wife to abuse, looked about the Portland House and found there a skinny little specimen of a man, his cook, Jim McFadden. Poor Mr. McFadden must have made the terrible mistake of assuming Mr. Turk needed some consolation and uttered some remark along the lines of: "Aw, Jim. Yer better off without some harpy screeching in yer ear." To which remark Mr. Turk responded with fists like hammers, beating poor Mr. McFadden into a bloody pulp. Mr. McFadden was scraped off the pavement and sent to the hospital, while Mr. Turk was marched off to police court.

Abigail Scott Duniway, supreme suffragette and publisher of the *New Northwest*, took the opportunity to open both barrels on Mr. Turk, as did the *Oregonian*, whose remarks Abigail Scott Duniway was happy to include in her text.

> *The ruffian Turk, who, after maltreating his wife so that she could not live with him, advertised her as having left his "bed and board without just cause or provocation," is again prominently brought into notice by his brutality. He got into a fight on last Sunday afternoon at his sailor boarding-house [sic] with his steward, James McFadden, and after knocking him down, kicked and stamped his prostrate body, mutilating him in a most horrible manner. As usual, the miserable coward attacked a little man, McFadden being light and sickly, while his bestial employer is robust and healthy. The injured victim is under the care of surgeons, while his assailant is out under $500 bonds.* [21]

The article continued for some paragraphs reviling the likes of Turk and all wife-beaters. A few days after this was printed, Jim Turk went down to Abigail Scott Duniway's office and declared that he had been ill treated in the article. He declared that he had thumped Mr. McFadden because he had "grossly insulted Mrs. Turk." Jim and Kate might separate many times, and often with violence, but they always came back to each other like an old habit.

Chapter 2
THE GRANT FAMILY OF ASTORIA

On Christmas Day in 1878, several handfuls of passengers from San Francisco disembarked at Astoria, Oregon, along with a cargo of U.S. mail, cases of whiskey and cartons of other sundries for the few merchants operating in this rain-drenched outpost.[22] Among the passengers was a large family, well dressed and looking very much like the family of a banker or other prominent citizen. Besides the mother and father, there were eight children, ranging in ages from a babe in her mother's arms to handsome lads approaching manhood. The younger children were unusually well mannered for youngsters traveling on Christmas—the one day of the year when a child wants to be indoors by a cozy fire. The matriarch of this tribe was a woman of interesting appearance, whose auburn hair and dark, intelligent eyes made her seem a decade younger than her forty-one years. She was obviously a strict and loving mother whose children, even the older boys, gave her both affection and obedience. The fact that she was born Irish was plainly to be seen in her appearance, her brogue and her name—Bridget, taken from the famous Celtic saint on the wild frontiers of ancient Christendom. Her husband, Peter Grant, was a handsome man of forty-eight years, stoic in his appearance but with a slight twinkle about the eyes. When he spoke, which was rarely, it was with the even thicker Gaelic brogue of a Cape Bretoner. His hands were the strong and knotted hands of a fisherman, and his posture was that of a lord. It was apparent to the other men aboard the launch, carrying the passengers from the steamer across the rough waters of the Columbia River to the Astoria wharves, that this man

"A Glance at Astoria, Oregon." *From* The West Shore *(1881)*.

was lord in the loving eyes of this lady, and of that fact each man could be quietly envious.

This tribe of eight children was not the entire reckoning of the Grant family. The eldest daughter, Mary, had recently married a ship's captain turned stevedore, a man named Richard Lemon. Captain Lemon was now famous on the docks of Astoria and upriver at Portland for hiring gangs of longshoremen and riggers who could load a vessel quickly and efficiently—a turnaround that saved the merchants and shippers money. Even though he and his young wife had been in the area but a short time, his bright personality and his willing participation in everything from baseball to judging boat races landed him the nickname "Our Dick."

Like many of those in the maritime trade on the lower Columbia, Captain Lemon was uncertain whether he should be an Astorian or a Portlander. The area was growing by leaps and bounds, and no one could say for certain which hamlet or town would one day receive the blessing of a transcontinental railroad, making it the seaport of Oregon. Mary had sung the praises of Astoria to her parents, a town she loved and knew her mother and father would love as well. Eventually, Captain Lemon would put his money on Portland, but from the very first, even as she stepped off of the launch and on to the rough-cut planks of the Astoria docks, Bridget Grant saw a place big enough for her family to prosper and small enough for her to reign as foremost among the ladies of the town.

The Grant family had come from Gloucester, Massachusetts, where Peter had been captain of a fishing smack. The Grants managed to save enough to purchase a saloon on Front Street, an income that Peter managed to extend by offering his services as a "master mariner."[23] The work was hard and steady, but it was clear that in Gloucester there was not enough business, either in fishing or in setting up whiskeys, to improve the fortunes of six growing boys. They sold the fishing smack and the saloon for a good price and left for the other side of the world, where a Celt had as good a chance as a purebred Anglo-Saxon to make his mark.

An elderly Bridget Grant (around 1900). *Courtesy of the Clatsop County Historical Society, Astoria, Oregon, photo CCHS 5597ooG.*

The Astoria that the Grant family came into that Christmas Day was a town of about 2,500 souls— loggers, sawmill workers, salmon fishermen, cannery workers (mostly Chinese), merchants, saloon keepers and prostitutes by the score. It was a rough place, with a total of seventy saloons, but the strong-spirited and handsome Bridget Grant was rougher, in her way. Her sons were as disciplined as any graduating military cadets so that by the time they reached an age where such temptations, as were plentiful in this frontier town, were within their reach, they knew better. No son of Peter and Bridget Grant would ever drink debilitating liquors in excess, gamble away hard-earned money or infect himself with the body-and-soul-destroying diseases brought on by whoring. They were also trained to fight for every dime that was due them. Bridget knew how to turn a tide to her favor and, when necessary, how to use the courts to do so.

Shortly after their arrival in Astoria, the Grant family had resumed a life on the Pacific Coast that mirrored, somewhat, the one they had lived in Gloucester. Peter purchased a fishing boat, with all its gear, and the family lived in quarters near the wharves with extra rooms to accommodate sailors.

Astoria, the Columbia River and the Columbia Bar panorama. Photographer unknown. *Author's collection.*

The Grant residence and boardinghouse was on land they purchased directly on the waterfront, seventy-five by fifty feet reaching down past the tide line. Here they erected a dwelling large enough for themselves, with room left over to take in sailors. Peter (the father) set about fishing, and all was fairly quiet for several years, with the exception of some minor lawsuits with local merchants. Like all the buildings, and even the streets, on or near the waterfront, their house was built on pilings above the tide line. The 1880 census shows that by that time, Peter considered himself a "hotel keeper," and Bridget was listed as "keeping house." Alex, the oldest son at twenty-one, is listed as "hotel waiter." John (Jack) Grant, nineteen, calls himself a "fisherman," and his brother Peter, seventeen, is listed as "laborer." The rest of the children were at school. One can imagine a jolly time could be had as a sailor boarding at the Grant house. The boys all gained a reputation as competent sportsmen. The brothers had reputations for being well liked and personable, and few are the sisters of large families who couldn't match their brothers in humor and antics.

In late November 1881, the elder of the Grant family was on the wharf near his dwelling untangling fishing nets. One of the nets in which his foot was entangled slipped over the edge of the wharf, and Peter was pulled into

the current, where he drowned. His body was taken to Portland, where he was laid to rest, with due ceremony, in St. Mary's Cemetery in East Portland. The sorrowing widow, Bridget Grant, found herself thrust into the position of being responsible for a house full of young men and children. Alex, the oldest, was also the least ambitious but did the best he could to act as head of the household. At his mother's prompting, he took the members of the Astoria city council to court, claiming the wharf was unsafe, as it had no railings. The case would eventually be lost, with the court finding in the defendant's favor.

For a number of years following the tragedy, Mrs. Grant was unable to abide looking out the window at the spot where her husband had met his death. She moved to Portland early in 1882, setting up a sailors' boardinghouse at 47 B Street, where she would live for the next five years. Here she and her sons worked together with the house in Astoria, gathering in deserters and shipping landlubbers. Both houses wore the name "Grant House," and both houses kept a low profile, rarely, if ever, doing things to bring themselves to the attention of lawmen or newspaper reporters.

Astoria was already getting a bit of a reputation for shanghaiing. One of the first shanghaiers was a man named James Cook, who tried to get the city to license sailors' boardinghouse runners so his competition would be lessened. Cook was an unsavory fellow who operated an opium den for the pleasure of his Chinese customers. Astoria's Chinese population at the time was not officially counted but rivaled or exceeded that of the white population. He was unable to contend with the rising competition in the trade of "shipping sailors."

In the early part of the 1880s, the main boarding master of Astoria (and Portland) was Jim Turk, who was sometimes in business with J.P. Betts, then an Astoria stevedore. Betts would have his hand in many other affairs and would become the shipping master of Portland and city constable in the 1890s.

One of the other older Astoria sailors' boardinghouses was the Liverpool House on First Street, between Lafayette and Washington. It was run by a Portland boxing promoter and sportsman named Mark M. Dee and the muscular Dick McCarron. Dee would become prosperous enough to open the Turf Exchange Bar at 124 First Street in Portland. He would then rise in fame to become the manager for the world famous pugilist, John L. Sullivan.[24] Jack Grant would sometimes work as a runner for this house.

A widow named Laura McCormack, a close friend of Mrs. Grant, ran the Hamburg House, a hotel on Water Street. This she ran with her daughter Sophie and an overly large Scandinavian fellow named August Iverson. All the establishments would use some of the local punks and jailbirds as runners.

In July 1883, Hume's sawmill, above the O.R.&N. Co. dock, caught fire—a fire that spread quickly along the wooden streets. Before the day was through, one-quarter of the city had burned to the ground, including the Astoria Grant House. With typical West Coast enthusiasm, the rebuilding began immediately, even though much of the town was uninsured. The Grant House was rebuilt and bore a respectable (for Astoria) appearance, as though it were a regular boardinghouse for commercial travelers.

One of the strangers to come into Astoria after the fire was a pugilist from back east. He saw a good thing in the sailors' boardinghouse racket and took to crimping like a fox takes to chasing chickens. He would later open a sailors' boardinghouse on First Street between Benton and Lafayette. He was a big, handsome fellow, with large brown eyes and a boyish smile. His name was Larry Sullivan.

Chapter 3

MR. LAWRENCE MALACHI SULLIVAN COMES TO TOWN

L arry Sullivan was a St. Louis–born pugilist, lately from Scranton, Pennsylvania, with a moderate reputation but an impressive pedigree. He was the nephew of the great John L. Sullivan, a man who was practically worshiped by every cigar-chomping, whiskey-guzzling, sports enthusiast from coast to coast. Larry carried himself like a prizefighter, and he had a mouth on him that gave him plenty of opportunity to practice his profession in an impromptu fashion. In September 1885, he was brought to Portland, having been offered $250 to help train Portland's pugilistic champion, James Reilly, for a fight with another local champion, Dave Campbell. Not long before the fight, Reilly and Sullivan had a falling out, making it so that Sullivan had

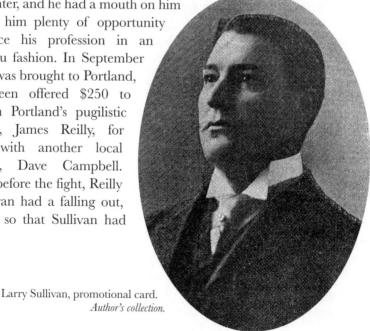

Larry Sullivan, promotional card.
Author's collection.

to look for other sources of income. He soon discovered that easy money could be made working as a "runner" for Jim Turk or some of the other sailors' boardinghouses encouraging indigent fellows to become sailors. All that was required was befriending some sailor or fortune seeker and talking them onto the steamboat under the pretext of money to be made in Astoria. Sullivan could see that Oregon was a sore place for suckers, but for a man with strength of character and cunning, it could be a gold mine.

In the contest for which Sullivan had trained Reilly, Campbell was triumphant, causing Sullivan to go about disparaging all the local talent, declaring that he could "lick anyone on the West Coast" (or words to that effect). A fight was in the works pitting a triumphant Campbell against a national middleweight champion, Jack "Nonpareil" Dempsey.[25] News of this fight circulated rapidly throughout the lower Columbia region, and any blood sport enthusiast or gambler who was able would spend his last dime to attend.

Another local champion, Tom Ward, had heard of Sullivan's boast and took him at his word, challenging him to fight at the Campbell-Dempsey event as a second feature. Sullivan was slow to respond, causing the *Oregonian* to print the following:

> *Ward thinks that Sullivan's powers lie in his capacity to use foul language, in which art he is the peer of any other blackguard in the state at this time…Sullivan, in addition to being ignorant of the abc's of pugilism, is entirely destitute of "sand."[26] In the language of the street, Sullivan "can't fight nothing," and the sooner he makes tracks for his Pennsylvania home the better the community will be pleased.[27]*

Sullivan would be laughed back to Scranton if he didn't stand up to that sort of public humiliation. The challenge was accepted, and it was determined that the fight would be "bare knuckles to the finish, London prize ring rules, to be fought in the same ring immediately after the Dempsey-Campbell fight."[28] The purse was $250 a side, and the date was set for All Saints Day, the second day of November. It would be a fight that was remembered by sports writers long into the twentieth century and even beyond. To circumvent city and county laws against boxing matches, the fight was to be carried out at a meadow on the Washington shore of the Columbia River.

On that morning, before dawn, a crowd of hundreds of men gathered at the steamboat dock on Front Street to board the fleet of steamboats churning the waters beside the wharves into a froth. At 7:00 a.m., the whistles began to blow, and one by one, the steamboats departed. The

A gathering of steamboats. *Washington State Archives, AR-07809001-ph005051.*

Fleetwood, City of Sellwood, New York and the *Calliope* loaded with hundreds of excited men and boys steamed downriver to a simple farm belonging to a man named Specht in Washington Territory. There a makeshift wharf was prepared, and the meadowland was large enough for the crowd, far from the long arm of authorities.[29]

From downriver at Astoria came the steamer *Clara Parker*, carrying about one hundred passengers. Men and boys braved the rough November currents of the Columbia to cross in rowboats and canoes from the Oregon side as far away as St. Helens. From the surrounding farms, they arrived on horseback. All told, there were about one thousand men and boys and, according to the *Oregonian*, "several women—one from Portland, very well disguised as a boy, with a skull cap drawn to the ears, and her coat buttoned closely around the neck. A gossamer storm coat helped much to conceal her identity."

The steamboats lined up, going out from the small wharf so the passengers needed to pass from steamboat to steamboat before disembarking. The sky was typical for November, with ragged low clouds, and the meadow was damp from rain. The sawdust that had been ordered for the ring area had not come, but the show would continue regardless. Just as Dempsey and Campbell were stripped and ready to begin, the sky opened with a drenching rain—albeit brief, followed by a sun break.

At about half past noon, the match began, Queensbury rules, with three-ounce gloves. There was a purse of $1,000 per side with the winner taking 65 percent and the loser 35 percent, but an untold fortune in the many tens

Jack "Nonpareil" Dempsey, world champion boxer, died in Portland 1895, promotional card. *Author's collection.*

of thousands was bet on the match by boxing fans near and far. The match went for three rounds before Campbell missed a hard swing at Dempsey and slipped to the ground. Before he got fully to his feet again, he was knocked cold, with a broken nose and covered in his own blood.

That afternoon, at 2:10 p.m., Larry Sullivan and Tom Ward met in the middle of the mud hole purported to be a ring. The rules, London prize ring rules, were made to fit the tastes of the brutal rogues of East London. They called for bare knuckles and allowed grabbing, wrestling and even spiked shoes (within limits). The fight could only end with a man down, unable to rise, or if broken up by riot or police action. As the crowd looked on—mostly cheering for Campbell—the two men shook hands in an amiable way and began to circle each other. Ward was the more muscular of the two, though shorter than Sullivan, who, fleshy and pale, seemed more like an overgrown schoolboy than a prizefighter.

From that moment on, Sullivan proved the mockery in the *Oregonian* wrong—he most certainly had "sand." The fight seemed to the spectators as almost endless, as it continued on and on through seventy-seven rounds—each round contributing more and more blood to the bruised bodies of the fighters, blood mixing with the wet earth, turning the mud a deeper and deeper red. Each round was much like the last: a circling, a "blow or two, then a clinch, then a desperate struggle, then a fall, Ward generally on top."[30]

Not long into the fight, one of Sullivan's eyes was swollen shut, and the other side of his face had taken on the appearance of a beef kidney in the butcher's shop. Ward had received several brutal blows to his face, causing the blood to flow freely in streams, coloring his chest and arms crimson. There were endless cries of "Foul! Foul!" as the men gouged and kicked at each other, trying to inflict as much damage as possible on the other man. Sullivan was getting the worst of it nearly from the start, and the sympathies of the crowd were against him. In his corner, though, was a man of the same Irish blood that Sullivan was spilling so freely from his wounded body—Jack Dempsey, whispering in his ear, encouraging and enraging him, as only an Irish warrior can do for his comrade in battle.

At the end of each round, Sullivan would lurch, almost drunkenly, to his seat, making the crowd think the end was near or that he would never rise from the spot. Then Dempsey would work magic on him like a shaman, and when "Time!" was called, Sullivan would slowly rise like some behemoth and lunge into the battle once more.

Sullivan at last sat down exhausted, and the catcalls and jeers from Ward and his followers had no effect. Dempsey called out that there was no water left to wash Sullivan's face, to help revive him. The referees said to use mud, which Dempsey did. Then the mud-covered, blood-soaked specter of Larry Sullivan stood up like a trembling fir tree hit by the woodsman's axe. The referees called out for him to come to the center—he obeyed like a sleepwalker, where he was met by Ward, who summoned up enough strength for some blows. This was followed by a groping clinch in which Sullivan managed to get his fingers into Ward's eyes. The referees were screaming "Foul!" as they pried his fingers loose. The fight was given to Ward on a foul.

The reporter noted, "The spectators had long been tired and disgusted, and very many of them said they never wished to see a prize fight again." Sullivan may not have won the fight, but he had secured the respect of all who witnessed the ordeal.

Chapter 4

THE PALMY DAYS OF JIM TURK

PALMY DAYS

When in later years, before the Great War, and before memories faded and the old waterfront was utterly forgotten, the Portland harbor of the 1880s would be recalled as the "palmy days of Jim Turk."[31] In those days, men stood back with amazement—or horror—to observe a man with no conscience to hinder him, a man without fear and a man with ample means to do either good or harm. Had he not been crippled by one degrading vice, he may have become governor of the state. He ran for mayor of Astoria and lost, but not because he wasn't capable of running things—when he was sober. Alcohol destroyed him at every juncture. It destroyed his wife, whom he loved deeply (in spite of everything), and eventually, all else—his wealth, his children, all burned by distilled spirits of ethanol taken into the body as a beverage for pleasure. James Turk and his entire family were ideal examples of why prohibition was established in Oregon four years before the rest of the country.

Turk was not a fellow easy to be entreated but one who warred openly with competitors (as they arose), with his wife, with obstinate sailors, with ships' officers and with officers of the law. He was a frequent passenger aboard the steamboat *R.R. Thompson* as he moved back and forth between his sailor's home in Portland and his boardinghouse in Astoria, strutting and champing his cigar like an adjunct general on the battlefield. It was his business to squeeze the last penny out of any half-starved, bug-eyed fool stupid enough

Steamboat *R.R. Thompson*. *Washington State Archives, AR-07809001-ph005052.*

to become a sailor. As the saying went among ships' captains, "The fool of the family goes to sea as surely as the goose goes to the mill pond." Turk was there to collect his dues, the tax that fools owed to the wise. He would take as much as the fools were willing to give.

For some reason, Jim Turk was also of the mind that he deserved a place of respect alongside the other business leaders, and he was quick to defend himself when attacked. When, in September 1880, the *Portland Daily Standard* published an article detailing some of Turk's "shanghaiing" practices, Turk fired off a response to the *Oregonian* declaring, "Should I ever so far forget all principles of honor as to 'shanghai' men, my business would soon be ruined, as it is well known that seamen fight as shy of a professional crimp as the devil does of holy water."[32]

The earnestness of this plea may convince someone unaware of the way the maritime industry worked, but if sailors were "shy of the professional crimp," then why were there sailors' boardinghouses in most ports, complete with all manner of crimp? The fact remained that crimps (with the compliancy of ships' captains) ran the business in most ports.

It is an abiding mystery why a man who was instantly wealthy would continue in a business so fraught with difficulty as "shipping sailors." Turk must have enjoyed the life of a crimp and enjoyed it so much that

Postcard depicting a steam tug bringing a vessel into Portland Harbor. *Author's collection.*

he continued on even when all need to do so was removed. He must have enjoyed the feeling of power it gave him to change men's lives so forcefully—taking in penniless strangers and turning them into seafarers, buying and selling sailors like cattle. He is portrayed in the press as being like a roaming predator, itching for a fight. His fat bankroll backed up his fat fists, making him a very difficult man to prosecute in a city where the payola went all the way to the top. Most offenses were dealt with swiftly by a police court judge. In the police court, offenses that today would bring stiff prison sentences—such as assault with a deadly weapon—were taken care of with relatively small fines.

The Lawsuit over "Turk's Nefarious Trade"

On July 28, 1882, the *Oregonian* got into the act and published an article titled "Turk's Nefarious Trade,"[33] which told the tale of his "shanghaiing" and how he even stooped so low as to rob sailors of their necessary clothing. It told the tale of a poor Dutchman who spoke only a few words of English. Turk's agent in Astoria had sold the Dutchman (at the high price of forty dollars) an outfit of clothes and boots but said he wouldn't deliver it until he got the blood money from the captain. Going on board as the ship was ready to sail, the Dutchman was told he could collect his outfit from the captain—which was a lie. The ship went to sea, and the poor fellow had to spend the next several months in thin clothes, without boots. The readers were appalled at this callousness, and the name of Jim Turk was now mud, if it had not been before.

Instead of ignoring the slight, as he usually did, Turk, being flush with cash from his departed uncle, found a lawyer and sued the *Oregonian* for libel—a move that opened him up for a higher level of ridicule than he could have anticipated. As a bully, he was not used to being on the receiving end, and the normally hesitant *Oregonian* started to dish it out with regular humorous jabs from many directions. One of these came in the month following the announcement of the lawsuit.

Living in Portland, for a season, was a poet of humorous verse, V. Hugo Dusenbury, whose work appeared regularly in *Puck*, America's foremost humor magazine, whose byline was, "What fools these mortals be." The *Oregonian* printed a rather lengthy Dusenbury poem titled "The Downfall of Jim Turk," which began with the words:

At midnight in his boarding-house [sic],
Jim Turk was dreaming of the hour
When editors in suppliance bent,
Should tremble at his power:

and ended thus:

Strike—till the last cockroach expires,
Strike—each and every man he hires,
Strike—for they all are mammoth liars,
No Turks in Oregon![34]

Following this bit of humor, a reporter detailed the trials and tribulations that the Turk family had faced in the week past under the title "A Busy Brood: A Sketch of the Every Day Life of the Celebrated Turk Family." Calling them "chronic brigands," he outlined the remarkable number of run-ins with the law members of the family had in the preceding week.

If there is one thing a bully hates, it is being mocked. Turk's protests at being labeled "crimp" and "shanghaier" had fallen on deaf ears. His lawsuit for defamation against the *Oregonian* had made him the object of derision in ways he had never anticipated. No one within the reach of his fists was laughing, but the rest of the city either ignored the doings of the lower classes, scoffed or feigned outrage. In November 1882, the case was moved ahead to the end of February. At that time, a jury found in favor of the *Oregonian*.[35]

Less than a week following the lawsuit, Reverend Stubbs of the

Middle-aged James Turk. *Oregon Historical Society, OrHi 87961 (bb005648).*

44

Portland Seaman's Friend Society received a letter from a fellow sailors' chaplain in New York City. Reverend Stubbs turned the letter over to the *Oregonian*, which published it in full under the headline:

> *Shanghaied*
> *A Weak-Minded Boy of Eighteen Years*
> *Drugged and Shipped on Board a Vessel Bound for England*

The letter, printed in full, was introduced with these words:

> *Another instance of the devilish business, which is continually being carried on in this city, of drugging men and boys and putting them aboard ships, to recover consciousness when out at sea, where months of hardship and unwonted toil are before them, has just come to light.*

The article continued by recommending that the "rascally perpetrators of this kind of work" be driven from the wharves of Portland and Astoria and out of the state. Then followed the text of the letter:

"Jack Tar's Rough Work." *Brodie Collection, La Trobe Picture Collection, State Library of Victoria, H99.220/2373.*

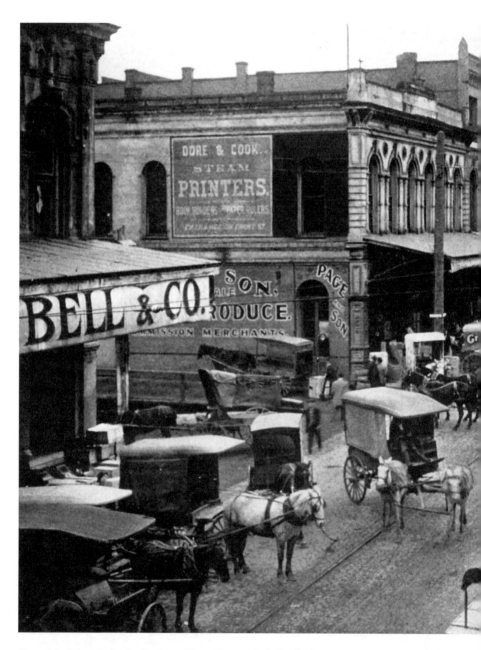

Postcard of the wholesale district on Front Street. *Author's collection.*

New York, Feb. 23, 1883
Dear Bro. Stubbs;
I am writing this in great haste, simply to get your help in a case of distress that has turned up here. A youth, I should say about 18, of very feeble intellect, helpless as he is harmless, came into our rooms a few days since, telling this story, or, rather, telling what I have put together in the following story; vis: He is Charles J. Birchard, from near Portland, Oregon, son of H.W. Birchard, a small farmer, living so that he gets his mail at Milwaukie. He was, sometime last March, in Portland sight-seeing, and persuaded in bad company to take a glass of cider, stupefied and in that state "shanghaied;" carried to Hull, England; begged and worked his way to Norfolk, Virginia, and to this port, where he has fallen into the care of our Sailor's Home, and now most pitifully cries to get back to his father and mother.

Can you find out and send as to the facts in this case and so prepare me for taking the next step. He is greatly to be pitied, poor fellow! friendless and deficient every way. He is no sailor—can do only such work as scrubbing deck, etc—is very ignorant and sleeps most of the time.

If he belongs to Portland and has friends there as he claims, I should be glad to know it and that as soon as may be. Whenever I see him in his forlorn state I am constrained to ask "Who maketh me to differ?" and for Christ's sake to do for him all I can. Please send me some word and oblige.
Yours as ever, Samuel H. Hall[36]

There were watchdogs to make sure shanghaiing didn't take place in Portland: Laidlaw's office for British vessels and the U.S. Shipping Commissioner's office or Customs office for American. There were harbor policemen and U.S. marshals. There were federal and state laws against practices such as boarding a ship without permission, enticing desertion, harboring deserting sailors and excessive advanced wages (not to mention kidnapping and drugging), and yet the evil persisted. It can't be said that officials such as Laidlaw were ever dishonest or profited from shanghaiing, but the same cannot be said for some other officials. J.P. Betts, the former Astoria stevedore, worked for decades as a quasi-official "shipping master." In Portland, his office was authorized to oversee the signing of ships' articles and the discharge of sailors for American vessels. Mr. Betts was elected as town "constable" for the Second Ward (North End), adding civil authority to his position.

Chapter 5

PIRATES OF THE PORT

Although Jim Turk pioneered the business of shipping sailors and tried to keep his hands on as many sailors as came through the two seaports, by the mid-1880s, it was far more than one house could handle. In the mist-shrouded, rain-soaked town of Astoria, there were more than a few hostels for the seafarer along the wharves and beside the rattling walls of salmon canneries. It was a town that smelled like fish guts, wood smoke and the delicious tang of Chinese food being prepared in dozens of kitchens. There was no Chinatown in Astoria. The Chinese population lived side by side with the Scandinavians, Anglos and Celts like the spirit world lives with the material—but who's to say which was which? The Chinese spoke of the whites as "ghosts," and the whites, for the most part, ignored the Chinese.

The people in Astoria involved in the business of shipping sailors seemed to do so without much in the way of infighting, causing the Portland papers to refer to them as a "nest of pirates." This may have been due to the influence of strong personalities, like Bridget Grant and her son Peter, or it may have simply been the community spirit of the much maligned port, but there was as much cooperation there as in Portland. Often a crew would desert a ship in Portland, to be replaced by a Portland boarding master, only to be stolen again in Astoria, making it necessary for the captain to buy another crew. This was not necessarily competition, for often the same boarding master was responsible for both events.

Larry Sullivan was identified as being a "sailor's boardinghouse runner" even by the time of his first pugilistic contest at the meadow on Specht's

"A Can of Salmon." Cannery of M.J. Kinney, Astoria, Oregon. *From* The West Shore *(1887).*

farm. It seems he was freelancing and may easily have worked for Jim Turk during that time. Turk's competitors in Portland at the time were Edward Mordant and Peter McMahon. Mordant was sentenced to the penitentiary for three years in 1880 for kidnapping and resumed where he had left off when released. Sam Wynn, a runner for Jim Turk, set up in business for himself but suddenly left town for his place on Whidbey Island. His wife ordered all the furniture sent north by train, and all that was left behind was an empty house and stacks of unpaid bills, including ninety dollars to the Chinese cook. J.W. Marr and his wife ran a place called the Virginia House and shipped sailors with the help of hired runners. At one time, they employed William Kelley, the brother of Joe "Bunco" Kelley, who, like his brother, could not keep himself from taking things that belonged to others. These are examples of the kind of crimps who have made a very small mark and disappeared into the anonymity of the boneyard. Sullivan may also have worked for the sailors' boardinghouse on Second Street run by Harry and Annie Lynch, a well-liked couple who managed to stay in business for many years without being hauled before the courts or being molested by either Jim Turk or someone in his service.

The past is ripe with surprises for those who turn over old stones and peer into the columns of old, yellowed newspapers. Just as Mr. Turk surprised the city by turning his sailors' boardinghouse into a bethel, so Mr. Sullivan surprised everyone by taking a job as a sailors' boardinghouse runner at the Mariner's Home. This is the same facility, originally established by the Seaman's Friend Society mission, that was built under the direction of Mr. H.W. Corbett, James Laidlaw, E. Quackenbush, John McCracken and others as a refuge for the "poor tar." It was to be a lighthouse of hope to the storm-tossed soul. The *Seaman's Friend* magazine described the dangers at sea as great, but the danger of land as far greater:

> *On the shore the dangers are of another kind, but often are far more deceitful and destructive. "Lewd fellows of the baser sort," loafers about the docks, "landsharks" hang along the shore, waiting for arrivals: and when the sailor plants his foot on terra firma he is on ground that may require his "sea-legs" even more than the deck. He needs to be firm-footed if he is to stand steady and upright amid the surges of temptation that now rise and roll around him. Drunken and depraved men will seek to lead him astray; and amid the seductions of the "grogshops," and the entangling snares of the "strange woman," how shall the sailor, set free from the restraints of duty or subordination, and with every opportunity to sin, keep himself from the ways of transgression?[37]*

The society built a lovely Mariner's Home facility in the North End in 1882 under the direction of Chaplain Stubbs, who had been sent to Portland by the society in 1877. The new facility was intended to provide an alternative to the boarding masters, a place where a sailor could restore his soul and body while waiting to ship out. The scheme never worked. The boarding masters had the sea captains cowed. They knew that if they used the Mariner's Home, they would have their crews stolen away and not replaced. Another factor causing sea captains to shun the Mariner's Home was that many, if not most, of the captains were able to turn a profit by buying a new crew for less than the money coming to them from the desertion of the old crew.

Some years later, in a consular report, the British vice-consul James Laidlaw would explain the situation in these words:

> *I have often found it difficult to induce masters of British vessels to engage independent seamen, requiring in many cases no advances and who are outside of the crimps' houses. I have even known them refuse to take men who were, in charge of the consulate, alleging that if they did so the boarding-house [sic] keepers would refuse to furnish the rest of the crew. I do not consider the excuse valid; such threats might be made, but it is extremely unlikely they would be carried out. Some time ago the Mariners' Home, a respectable institution*

owned and operated by the Seamen's Friend Society, had to be closed because the British shipmasters, as a general rule, preferred to patronize notorious crimps, and would not take seamen from the home.[38]

Before the Mariner's Home closed, there was quite a shuffle. Chaplain Stubbs was appointed to the position of U.S. shipping commissioner in January 1885.[39] When he resigned two months later, he became the first person to resign a federal commission in the state of Oregon.[40] This brief season of dealing directly with the subterfuge and evil tricks of the crimps must have made his gray head grayer. He then moved to the Puget Sound, leaving his son in charge—an assignment that was very equally short-lived. Eventually, the Mariner's Home tried to make a go of it, shipping sailors at reasonable rates, under the direction of a man named D.W. Pratt. Pratt was the man who hired Larry Sullivan, and under Pratt's guidance, money was being made, though not necessarily by the Mariner's Home.

In June 1888, James Meade, a sailor aboard the British four-masted bark *Clan Buchanan*, wrote a letter to the president of the Seaman's Friend Society in New York (also published in the *Oregonian*) detailing the evils that a sailor faces when coming to Portland. The letter was mailed from Havre, France, and signed by all the crew members. He described the experience two of the men in the crew had with the Mariner's Home:

I have one thing to say, pertaining to the Mariners' Home, in Portland, as there are two men on this ship who lived there while in Portland, and until they told me different, I was under the impression that seamen's accounts were honestly made out, prior to their leaving, and in case of not owing the full amount of their advance to the home, that the balance should be handed over to them; but I find this is not the case, for it is the same there as it is in a boarding house [sic], let a man be there one week or one month, still he does not see the balance of his advance. I should most certainly have thought it would have been different in the Home, but it is not so. The boarding masters, Mr. Pratt, the manager of the Mariners' Home included, are combined together and their sole object is to rule over captains and seamen visiting Portland and Astoria, with a despotic sway, which captains requiring crews and seamen wanting ships, have no power to resist.[41]

Whether or not the printing of this letter helped Mr. Pratt decide to move on to better things isn't known, but at about this time, he formed a company for the purpose of shipping sailors in Astoria, using a boardinghouse

The vessel *Clan Buchanan. Brodie Collection, La Trobe Picture Collection, State Library of Victoria, H99.220/4186.*

named the Manchester. This company continued until November of that year, when it was purchased by Larry Sullivan, Peter Grant and Joe Baker. Baker was one of those good-natured punks who are always nearby, ready to second in a prizefight or beat up a sailor—anything for a friend. He even sailed Jim Turk's sailboat, *Young Turk*, for him in Astoria boat races. But Joe Baker wasn't quite the stuff—more like a thug or a sailor—he didn't look good in a suit. Before long, the firm bore the name "Sullivan, Grant Bros. & McCarron" and was made up of Larry Sullivan, Peter, Jack and sometimes Alex Grant and tall, good-looking, athletic, Richard McCarron. They all looked good in suits.

Chapter 6

THE SHANGHAIING OF
DARIUS NORRIS

A cross the four-mile-wide mouth of the Columbia from Astoria, a thin crust of peninsula stretches north for a distance of about twenty-six miles, separating the Pacific Ocean from the mudflats and oyster beds of Willapa Bay. Toward the top is the old town of Oysterville, and near the bottom is Ilwaco and the ferry terminal where boatloads of beach-goers passed through during the summer months, heading for the hotels and campgrounds of Long Beach. In 1885, a large acreage on this peninsula, south of Oysterville, was owned by a man named Darius Norris. This land, which had been considered almost worthless when it was acquired years earlier by Darius's father, was now worth a small fortune and was coveted by others.

Like many settlers in the region, Norris was land rich and money poor. He lived with his elderly mother in the hamlet of Chinook, Washington Territory, across Bakers Bay from Astoria. When the money jar got low, he made his way over to the Astoria side to work running cannery machinery or longshoring. The 1880s had brought a flood of new immigrants to the area, causing a rise in land speculation. This made the Norris property a bone of contention in the Norris family. Darius's mother thought the land should stay in the family, but his sister Mary thought it was foolish not to sell it while the price was high, and she wasn't shy to talk about these affairs in public. She even went so far as to discuss the situation with a shyster lawyer by the name of L.G. Carpenter.

There was, at the time, a man living north of Chinook, in the lonesome wilds at the mouth of the Cedar River, who also bore the name Norris. This man, Peter Norris, lived with his wife and five children on a ranch where he raised some cattle and did some logging around the area, getting by with the help of a ranch hand named Browning. If the story told by locals is true, it seems Browning had a wife who caught the eye of Peter Norris. This resulted in several heated incidents between the two men. One day in August, Browning told his wife that he was going out berry picking. That afternoon, two gunshots were heard by Mrs. Browning and by the members of the Norris family. Browning never returned home. A search party was collected from North Cove, the closest settlement to the Norris ranch. After many days of searching, Browning's partially decomposed body was found in an area that had recently been damaged by forest fire. Suspicion lay heavily on Peter Norris, but there was no proof, and since Mrs. Browning had left the area, no charges were brought against him. It may have been murder, or it may have been suicide, but it remained a mystery.[42]

At the beginning of March 1891, Darius Norris did as he had done before and headed across the Columbia to Astoria to work for a man named McGregor, running the plunger machine at his cannery during the fishing season. Since the salmon run had not quite started, Norris went longshoring at the Union Pacific dock. At the noon lunch break on March 14, Norris was walking across the dock when he was stopped by W.J. Barry, the Astoria chief of police. In later testimony, Norris would recount, in chilling detail, the events that followed:

> *I was walking across the dock he ordered me to stop and said:*
> *"Come with me, I have orders from Sheriff Turner of Pacific County to arrest you."*
> *I objected and told him to show me his warrant. He said:*
> *D—m you. I don't need a warrant; you come along down to jail or I will fill you full of lead.*
> *On the way down I begged him to let me get bonds, but he refused, and would not let me see any one. When we reached the jail, I was thrown in a dark cell and Barry told me I could get a couple of attorneys. I told him I wanted the Fulton Bros. and he said he would bring a couple of attorneys, and I must take the ones he brought, as he would have whoever he pleased, and didn't want Fulton. He told me that a Mrs. Browning had made a confession implicating me in murdering Browning, and said that men had gone over to Pacific county to search for Browning, and that I was in a very bad fix. He then brought C.J. Curtis and L.G. Carpenter to me for attorneys, and Carpenter told me I was in a pretty bad scrape and*

Astoria Rescue No.2 Hose Team. The coach, W.J. Barry, chief of police (and son-in-law of Bridget Grant), is center rear, and Peter Grant is to his left. *Courtesy of the Clatsop County Historical Society, Astoria, Oregon, photo CCHS image.*

must do just as Barry told me. He afterwards told me that if I would give Barry $400, I would be released. I told him I would not do it, and he left again, telling me to do just as Barry told me. Curtis did not have much to say, but told me he could fix it up so that I could get free. After Curtis and Carpenter had left, Barry came in and said that he was going to send me over to Sheriff Turner, in Pacific county, and then I would see how bad a fix I was in. I told him I was innocent and was not afraid to go over, and wanted him to send me then.

After I had been in jail five or six days, Carpenter came round with some papers and thrusting them through the cell window, told me to sign them. I could only see the bottom part of the papers, and asked him to let me read the rest. He would not do it, and told me to sign them quickly, as he could not get me out unless I did. I was so anxious to get out that I signed without thinking of their being so very important.

A few nights after this Barry came in about 9 o'clock and told me to go up to the scow where I had been living, near the Union Pacific dock, and get my blankets, as he was going to send me over to Sheriff Turner. I said if Turner wanted me he could furnish blankets for me. He took me out of the cell and told me to walk up to the scow and after getting my blankets there to get what things I had at Roger's fish market, and not to speak a word to anyone or attempt to run away or hide, or he would kill me instantly.

I started up the street and he followed not far behind and stood on the corner, near the Fishermen's Union office until I got my blankets and came out. He then came down the street with me, and when we reached Roger's fish market he crossed the street and stood in the dark alley between Sovey's saloon and Cooper's store and watched me until I came out. John Rogers was the last one of my friends I saw in Astoria, and I was afraid to tell him of my trouble for fear Barry would shoot me right there. When I came out I crossed the street and rejoined Barry, and he took me around on the back streets, and somewhere near the Astor house we met a man whom I recognized as Andrew Shoren. Barry told me to stand still, and he took Andrew to one side and talked to him several minutes, after which we went on down and finally turned and went down to the Liverpool sailor boarding-house [sic], near Kinney's cannery. We went over the net racks and came to a ladder which led down to the water, where a boat was lying. All the way down from Roger's Barry had been telling me that my life would not be safe if I ever came back again, and when we reached the ladder he said:

"D—m you, get in that boat and never come back again!"

There were two men in the boat; one was Larry Sullivan and the other was a rather tall man who I think was Joe Baker. They took me out to a ship lying in the stream abreast of the cannery. The ship, as I afterwards learned, was the Sierra Blanen [sic, Sierra Blanca][43] *bound for Dunkirk, France.*

When they put me aboard they told me that I had been signed under the name of John Smith and must not use my right name. I was put down in the hold the first night, and Frank Sweeny, a halfbreed, stood watch over me with a revolver, threatening to shoot if I made a move to escape. The next day he let me come up on the deck, but made me hide in the forecastle, and took my place working with the crew. He stayed aboard watching me until the vessel lifted anchor to go down to Sand island. Then he went ashore after telling me that the captain's orders were to shoot down the first man who attempted to go over the side when the vessel was at Sand island. I was around the deck, but could not get away, as the carpenter aboard the ship was watching me all the time. When we reached the mouth of the river I saw I was in for it and worked the best I could, but as four of the crew were shanghaied and knew nothing about the work, it was so hard on the rest of us that we were worked almost to death.[44]

The ship Darius Norris was shanghaied on board, Sierra Shipping Co. Ltd. bark *Sierra Blanca. Brodie Collection, La Trobe Picture Collection, State Library of Victoria, H99.220/3260.*

It was a fearful thing to be shanghaied under any circumstances, but to be blatantly done such an injustice by a law officer, sworn to uphold the peace, must have been even more disheartening. It wasn't long after Darius Norris was found to be missing that a disinformation campaign was started by the shyster L.G. Carpenter, who was also a newspaperman, once the editor of the *Saint Helens Columbian*. The plan was threefold: get money to line the pockets of W.J. Barry, get blood money for Larry Sullivan and get the deed to Darius Norris's property signed over to L.G. Carpenter. Before long, editors around the Pacific Northwest who needed to fill a little space in their pages would do so with an anonymous item received by mail. It read, "A sensational story comes from Astoria, Oregon about the running away of a man named Darius Norris, who fled to South America leaving $20,000 worth of property. It is claimed he was frightened off by enemies who knew of his complicity in a murder committed near Oysterville several years ago."[45]

The men involved in this escapade counted on confusion of the last name, Norris, with that of a man strongly suspected of murder to be a sufficient smokescreen. Norris, however, was well known as a trustworthy fellow and was unrelated to the area where the crime was committed, so the ruse backfired. Though it was a fairly easy prospect to shanghai a vagrant or an itinerant worker, such as a miner or logger, when a local man with family connections went missing, it always created a sensation. I doubt that the South America story carried much weight in Astoria, but at least it took the attention away in other regions. By this time, the local population was getting wary of their chief of police, and even though he carried the plan off in great secrecy, suspicions were undoubtedly aroused in his direction.

Darius Norris was off on a miserable voyage lasting many months. He recounted how four members of the crew (besides himself) were shanghaied and knew nothing of the difficult and arduous tasks aboard ship. In a vessel the size of the *Sierra Blanca*, this would have been a quarter of the crew that were nearly worthless, deadweight in a passage that tried even skilled mariners to their fullest. To make things go from torment to torture, somehow the supply of citrus juice ran out, and most of the crew developed scurvy. The ship was actually headed for Liverpool for orders, so it must have been depressing beyond words to be anchored in the river Mersey, within sight of Liverpool, and unable to go ashore until the vessel moved on to Dunkirk. By then it was the end of July.

Once across the Atlantic, the sailor "John Smith" received letters from home. The first was from the shyster Carpenter, advising him to go to Australia and never go home again. He said to do this "no matter what

"Heave ho!" *Brodie Collection, La Trobe Picture Collection, State Library of Victoria, H99.220/2375.*

your friends may say," for he would surely be killed the day he returned to Astoria. The second letter was from the other lawyer, C.J. Curtis, advising him to return immediately to claim his property that was in dispute since he had signed it away to Carpenter. This came as a shock and a surprise to Norris, as he had no idea the papers he had signed in jail were signing over the deeds of his property.

When it came time for Norris to receive his pay, he discovered that Larry Sullivan had been paid $140 blood money and $40 advance for his labors. All he had coming to him after that was less than £3 sterling. He then went to the United States consul to complain but could find no one among the bureaucrats who would even give him the pleasure of recounting his woes. The same outcome was met by the other men shanghaied aboard his vessel.

Norris then took passage to London, along with one of the crew members of the *Sierra Blanca*, expecting to earn their way to New York aboard a steamship carrying cattle. The emaciated men did not appear to be fit enough for the labor and were rejected. Nearly penniless and desperate, Norris then applied with Captain Davis of the American bark *Recovery*, who took pity on the poor man and hired him for a trip to New York.

Meanwhile, back at home, the letter he sent in reply to C.J. Curtis was causing a stir in the newspapers, printed verbatim, even though it was nearly incomprehensible in places. It was enough to set things in motion. Charles May, a friend of Norris's from Astoria, set out by train to meet the *Recovery* when it came in to the port of New York. The vessel first docked for weeks at Fowye, in Cornwall, to take on a load of chalk ballast, before setting out on an uneventful voyage across the Atlantic.

The arrival at New York proved that the crimps of the Sullivan, Grant Bros. & McCarron firm had not been idle. They had obviously telegraphed some associates in New York apprising them of the situation, for while the *Recovery* sat in quarantine, crimps boarded the vessel looking for Norris by his real name and also by the name of John Smith, by which he was shanghaied. Through some small miracle, he was able to conceal himself while they were on board. Charles May had by this time arrived at New York and was able to hire a tug to go out to the vessel to retrieve Darius Norris. His arrival was a mixed blessing, for Charles May carried with him the grievous news that Darius's mother had died in his absence. This was the most hurtful of all the events connected to his shanghaiing, to be kept from his dying mother's side.

When Norris finally made it back to Oregon, his story was much in demand, except in Astoria, where contrary forces had been at work all the while he was away. His story, nearly verbatim, was published in the *Oregonian* under the heading: "All the Elements, Astoria's Sensational Story, Darius Norris Tells How He Was Shanghaied and Forced to Leave His Home and Family." With unsuppressed optimism, the *Oregonian* mentioned that Astoria's new chief of police, Clark Loughery, had started working up the case as soon as Norris was back in the States. The Norris article concluded by saying, "In bringing about this result, he has been assisted by Sheriff Smith, who, with Loughery, will enjoy the credit of running to earth the first shanghaiers against whom positive evidence has been secured."[46]

Norris looked at least ten years older than before he left. His face was gaunt and pale, and his body shook. Maybe if the perpetrators were brought to justice, there would be some reason or slight satisfaction for his tribulations. He put his face in his hands and sobbed, "They ruined my health, wronged my family, robbed me of my property, and killed my good old mother, while they were hounding me round the world where I couldn't be near her in her dying moments."[47]

L.G. Carpenter had gone to San Francisco just as the story was breaking, but not before hastily signing the property back over to the Norris family. W.J. Barry was arrested and released on bail. Oregon governor Sylvester

Pennoyer signed a warrant saying L.G. Carpenter was wanted to answer to kidnapping charges and the warrant was sent to the chief of police in San Francisco. When Barry came to trial in Astoria before a jury of his peers, he was promptly acquitted. He had also been arraigned on a charge of stealing Clatsop County tax money to the tune of $4,720 missing from his safe. He claimed the money had been stolen but not by him. When this came to trial, the ex-chief was once more acquitted by the jury.

When news of this reached San Francisco, the warrant against L.G. Carpenter was refused on grounds of "insufficiency," and he was set free. Shortly after this, W.J Barry was back on the Astoria police force.

This story resolved itself in a most unsatisfying manner, as did many other such tales. One can only guess at the reasons why so many blackguards were handed so many acquittals by so many juries in those days. I shouldn't wonder but that many of the members of the jury expected something for themselves in return, from either the accused or from his counsel. It may also be that many in the community approved of the much-rumored notion that Chief Barry got rid of local troublemakers by incorporating the help of local boardinghouse masters to shanghai them out of the Clatsop County jail.

Chapter 7

CITIZEN TURK

"Shamefully Treated"

From the time of James Turk's lawsuit against the *Oregonian* onward, he was given a new title in the press, that of "Citizen Turk," and his "dutiful" son, Charles, became "the dutiful," as though they were characters from one of those complex and intricately drawn comics of the nineteenth century. The name of Jim Turk had become well known in maritime circles around the globe as well, especially as his methods became more violent and greedy.

An example of the methods Turk used to swindle sailors can be seen in the tribulation of captain George W. Mundle, captain of the British bark *Garnock*. The day before he left Portland Harbor, the British schooner *Imperial* arrived, and a fair number of its crew abruptly deserted for Turk's boardinghouse. The next day, Captain Mundle made arrangements for a crew. Turk provided him with six sailors, the number he needed to round out his crew. All of the men signed the ship's articles, as required, and the ship moved downriver with the late evening tide. The next morning, Captain Mundle discovered he had six men who were now threatening to desert the ship—so, as was his right and duty, he clapped them in irons and kept them below as prisoners.

The captain examined the men to get to the bottom of their complaints. It seems they had spent only one night at Turk's boardinghouse, and he had charged them as though they had been there for many days, running up a large tab. He had also charged them for oilskins, clothes and liquor. They had no oilskins or extra clothes, not even the ones they had with them when they left the *Imperial*, and the liquor they swore had been drugged. Turk had kept the men's sea chests and charged them for articles of clothing they had not received. The men were clamoring to see the British vice-consul. The *Garnock*, however, was on a tight schedule and could not spare the time to sue in American courts for the affairs of mere seamen. The men were to be kept in chains until the vessel was across the bar and well out at sea, and then they would have no choice but to carry on. In this as well, the captain was within his rights.

His sympathies did lie with the men, however. He wrote in a letter to a friend in Portland:

> *I consider the men have been most shamefully treated, as I have seen the clothes they have, and I also have got four of their discharges from the* Imperial.
>
> *They only want to have some clothes, and are willing to go in the ship provided Turk is exposed to the authorities. They seem very good men, and I feel sorry for them for they have got absolutely nothing for them, for they have got absolutely nothing for their money. The captain of the* Imperial *says the men left his ship well clothed and with money.*[48]

This was not an isolated incident. If Turk, his son or any of his employees could steal the clothes off a sailor's back, they would do so without a second thought. These articles would then be sold to other sailors at high prices. It was a normal practice on British vessels for the captain to carry on board what was called a "slop chest." This chest, or collection of chests, was filled with necessities, such as tobacco and articles of clothing, to be sold to the crew. Usually, the captain's steward would open the store one evening each week. The items purchased there could usually be paid for by a tab to be deducted from the sailor's pay, but in the case of Captain Mundle of the *Garnock*, the men robbed by Turk were already in arrears for advanced pay.

The new decade brought to Citizen Turk's north section of the city an infusion of ruffians, scoundrels, bunco men, morphine fiends, dancing girls, prostitutes and any other undesirable character as roamed the earth in those "palmy" days. As rail travel finally came to the city, Portland was no longer at the end of the earth but merely the end of an exhausting train trip. In the East, newspapers and magazines touted the beauty and richness of this charming city of Portland to a readership that was often made up of rootless migrants, eager to blow off, like windblown dandelion seeds, to infest the greener pastures.

Often sailors went to sea with the poorest of clothing and footwear. *Airspy Collection, State Library of Victoria, H2012.59/90.*

The successful early settlers—the "first citizens," the sea captains, bankers, real estate speculators and commodity merchants—had constructed elegant homes and carriage houses along the north end of the city, between Couch Lake and the large and commodious Ash Street dock of the Oregon Steam Navigation Company. In Portland at that time there were no real slums, unless you count "Slabtown"—the shanties near the river built from refuse slabs from the lumber mills, mostly used to fuel steamboats. The exodus of the wealthy was abrupt and was caused by two things: one too many Willamette River floods and an infusion of riffraff surrounding their dwellings with unsightly "blind pigs and bagnios," to use the terminology of the day (unlicensed saloons and bawdyhouses).

The year 1883 brought about a remarkable exodus of the mansion class from this area, which would soon inherit the name "Bad Lands" or "Whitechapel" (lifted from Dickens's version of the infamous east end of London). The North End became the home of Liverpool Liz and dozens like her. It was an area smothered in clouds of soot and ciders from passing trains, the ash from the sawdust burners of a long line of sawmills lining the northwest riverbank and hundreds of home fires burning in hearth and stove. Like the ash that anointed the heads of penitents in Dickens's *Hard Times*, Portlanders in the North End had smudges on their celluloid collars and streaks on the washing hung out to dry. All this the wealthy citizens abandoned for the upper reaches of Nob Hill.

In the introduction to the 1884 Portland City Directory, this comment was made:

> *North Third and Fourth streets, which were the sites of our most elegant residences have been abandoned to business, and the denizens of that portion of the city have as completely changed in character as their surroundings. The blackberry pasture and forlorn waste of stumps in the western precincts have been reclaimed and improved almost magically, and for a half mile square in the former suburbs of the city at the north end the dwellings erected during 1883 may be called almost palatial.*[49]

The Turk family was at the center of this transformation, serving as a kind of dark balance to the wealth and prosperity provided the city by its newfound status as a seaport. The Turks were an ongoing drama, a "reality show" for the readers of newspapers, supported by nefarious characters like Bunco Kelley, Paddy "the Canary" Lynch and a sinister crimp named Mordant, to name but a few.

During this period, it was reported in the *Astorian* that Jim Turk was sued for shipping a blind man, an exploit that went pretty much unnoticed, overshadowed at the time by the attention-grabbing headlines of the famous Carrie Bradley murder with headlines like: "Drugged to Death!" and "Murdered in a Den of Fiends!"

It was also reported that he shipped (or "shanghaied") a dead man, which again was true or, at least, was reported as true in the newspapers, with the *Willamette Farmer* suggesting he get the "blue ribbon"[50] for it. The decade that began with such milestones held much promise—at least for crime reporters, lawyers and undertakers.

A MAN WHO WOULD SHANGHAI HIS OWN SON

Since the 1930s and 1940s, days when Stewart Holbrook stories appeared in the pages of the *Atlantic Monthly*, the *American Mercury* and the *Oregonian*, it has been an oft-repeated half-truth that Jim Turk shanghaied his own son. This tale, as told by Holbrook, has even appeared in history books. The way in which it was recounted by Spider Johnson to Stewart Holbrook was published verbatim in his 1933 series on shanghaiing written for the *Sunday Oregonian*.

> *Yes, Jim Turk shanghaied his own son. That is, he put the son aboard a vessel in Portland harbor, while the son was unconscious, and collected "blood money" from the ship's captain for delivering another seaman. The son had been drinking too much good liquor and associating with too many bad women, if I can rely on reports I have received from sources which I believe to be impeccable. Young Turk was put—unconscious, as I said—aboard a ship in Portland harbor, and he went down to the sea in a ship. He was away several months, and I guess the trip did him good. He came back cured of his former habits and is now a respectable and prosperous business man [sic] in a California city.*[51]

Spider Johnson claimed to be a sailor at the very end of the sailors' boardinghouse period and was a man unafraid of embellishment. Had Holbrook done a little fact checking and researched what was printed on the subject in the newspapers of the period, he would have discovered a more interesting story.

Jim Turk did indeed shanghai his own son—Charles, to be exact. Not only did he shanghai him once but more times than either of them could remember. Turk would shanghai his son any chance he got. He would sell him to a ship's captain for the going rate of blood money, usually about three months' wages at whatever rate was paid for the job he was filling. Then Charles would seem to be going along with the setup, perfectly happy, even looking forward to be heading back to sea. It would be necessary to throw suspicion off himself. As we have seen with Captain Mundle, a captain was quite willing to put men in irons if he suspected desertion was afoot. Many ships traveled beyond the Columbia bar with U.S. marshals or other constables on board to suppress desertion.

In the Turk's game, once the ship was heading downriver to Astoria, Charles (an expert swimmer) would leap overboard and head for the shore. He would then find his father and receive his cut of the bargain.

This trick worked repeatedly, until the fateful day of February 27, 1884. The British grain ship *Henry James* was loaded and ready to be moved downriver to the ocean. The captain, a man of wit and experience, had been in the port before, and once before he had lost three months' seaman's wages by signing on Charles Turk. The captain recognized Charles among the new crew members. He said nothing about it and acted as though he was in the dark. As soon as Charles was on board, however, and the tug was alongside, he clapped the young man in irons and put him below in a storeroom he used as a temporary brig.

One can only imagine the lad's disappointment—no, his agony—to be foiled like this! Ahead of him was a grueling 110 days (probably more) of rough seaman's work before seeing land again, and then he was faced with the difficulties of a return trip.

As the *Henry James* sat at anchor in Astoria waiting for the Columbia bar pilot, the captain made certain that the *Astorian* newspaper was informed that Charles Turk was among the crew. The ship then sailed with its load of wheat following its instructions: "Queenstown for orders." There would be no stopping at San Francisco and no solid terra firma beneath Charles Turk's feet until the Irish transfer port of Queenstown, near Cork, where most transatlantic route vessels went to receive telegraph orders from London for their European destinations.

Even though the tale told by Spider Johnson has become fixed in history books, the account here is the true one. It is backed up by an account published in the Salem, Oregon *Daily Capital Journal* and the one told by Jim Turk himself to the *Oregonian* in 1884. Charles had been missing for months, and since it was known he had sailed on the *Henry James*, it was assumed that he had been shanghaied by his father out of pure meanness. Jim Turk put the story straight in an item that ran in the July 26 *Oregonian*: "Jim Turk desires it stated that his son Charley was not shanghaied, but duly shipped as an able seaman. However, Charley didn't intend to go to sea, and wouldn't if the captain hadn't been wary enough to put him below hatches until they got outside."[52]

Furthermore, when Charles returned, he was not a "reformed California businessman" but continued working the trade with his father, eventually moving to Tacoma to set up a sailors' boardinghouse on the Puget Sound.

Many fabrications, such as the version of this story recounted by Holbrook, have become a part of the city's "fakelore" (as opposed to "folklore"), and many in recent years have been embellished to the point where they resemble a sort of combination of the exploits of Baron Von Munchausen and the Marquis de Sade—invented to amuse or frighten tourists in downtown taverns with dark basements.

In April of the following year, Charles Turk made his return home from sea known to readers of the *Oregonian* by the account of the savage beating of Lewis Gung, a German sailor. As it was reported, Gung was beaten for the misdemeanor of asking Jim Turk for fifty cents. According to the account of Gung, who showed up at the police station with "bruised, battered, and discolored features," once he had made the request for money, his arms were held by Jim Turk while Charlie beat him. The reporter's cynical conclusion to the story, based on countless previous events stated, "It's safe to bet, the sailor gets fined, and the Turks go free." This seemed to be the conclusion to most of their encounters with law enforcement.

Even young Frank Turk, a lad of about twelve at this time, as I can imagine, was busy with his urchin friends, pulling protection rackets on smaller kids at school. He is reported to have had his own brushes with law enforcement for using a baseball bat to pummel rocks through Slabtown windows.

Jim and Charles Turk were ruthless enough on their own, but they employed men who tended to be even more ruthless, less restrained and more inclined to end their days either behind bars or at the end of a rope. George Franklin, Thomas Ward, Paddy Lynch, Bunco Kelley and Dan Moran all worked for Turk at one time or another, but much as it was with the eunuchs employed by the infamous Nabobs of Istanbul, it was a dangerous thing to be close to the seat of power. All these men suffered for their association, but all were victims of their own passions, which would have led them to destruction with or without the likes of James Turk.

THE MURDER OF FREDRICK KALASHUA

Few cases brought the horror of the subterranean world of the sailors' boarding master to the surface quite like the murder of Fredrick Kalashua, a ship's carpenter and a Finn. As a ships' carpenter, he was a valuable commodity in the maritime world—the sort of fellow many captains tried to keep on board while the other sailors deserted. This grisly tale unfolded in July 1886.

The captain of the British ketch *Candidate*, on which Kalashua came to Portland, was a prudent man. He was also a captain who knew how the port worked, and the weaknesses of his men. As a precaution against losing his valuable ships' carpenter, upon arrival in port, the captain left sixty dollars with the British vice-consul's office as a sort of insurance, to be paid to Jim Turk, so that Kalashua would be returned to him when it was time for the *Candidate* to sail. This was most likely in addition to the tab Kalashua would run up. It is certain that the captain expected Kalashua to do a fair bit of drinking while in port, and rather than see him shanghaied, he sent him to stay at the boardinghouse with Turk as his protector, a job Turk expected his runners to assist him with, as he was in Astoria at the time.

The arrangement would have worked as planned but for two things: Turk had recently brought up to Portland from Astoria one of his runners, Dan Moran, a hoodlum with few brains and lots of brawn. Moran had been an Astoria problem child for years. He had already served two long stints in the state penitentiary in Salem, as well as numerous visits to the Clatsop County jail. It is not clear why Turk brought the lad to Portland, but it was a move he would regret. The other problem was with Kalashua, described in police reports as a large, powerful man. Kalashua was also a belligerent fellow who had some disagreement with the captain of the *Candidate*. On arrival at Turk's boardinghouse, he immediately put his name on the slate requesting that he be shipped on a different vessel.

On July 8, Moran spent the entire afternoon with Kalashua, moving from saloon to saloon. Around midafternoon, they happened upon Jim Turk, newly arrived by steamboat from Astoria. At the inquest, Turk said that he had asked Moran where he was going with the ships' carpenter. Moran had replied, in a whisper, that he was "going uptown to fix this fellow off."

It can be surmised from the reports that the *Candidate* was scheduled to sail with the rising of the early morning tide.[53] The belligerent Finn was not intending to be aboard, but Moran was going to play the oldest trick in the book on him. In the early evening, he took Kalashua to a saloon owned by

Painkillers and opiates were easily had. *Airspy Collection, Library of Congress,* H2012.59/90.

James Kelly.[54] By this time, Kalashua was feeling ill from all the alcohol. He refused to drink any more liquor but asked for a glass of soda water. Kelly then poured the soda water into a glass with a little sugar and, apparently, some morphine solution, at the request of Dan Moran.

By early evening, Kalashua was back at the Sailor's Home, where he refused supper but rather hung up his coat and went to sleep in the salon.

A little before 3:00 a.m., James Turk's alarm clock roused him. A horse cab would soon be arriving to take sailors to the *Candidate*, embarking with the high tide. Apparently, Turk was unaware of the extra measures his runner had gone to in making sure the contract with the *Candidate*'s master was met. Turk roused the house dishwasher and bookkeeper, a man named Casey, and told him to wake Kalashua. After a short while, Casey found Turk and told him that Kalashua would not wake up. Turk went in to the salon where Kalashua lay. He shouted in his ear and slapped him. Kalashua's head rolled in a manner that was sickening to behold.

"My God, what is the matter with the man?" Turk later testified were his words. He then sent for the local beat cop, an officer named Belcher. When Belcher arrived, his immediate opinion was that Kalashua had either been doped or poisoned, and Casey was sent to bring Dr. S. Parker, a pharmacist from the neighborhood. Casey later testified that Dr. Parker had said, "I'll go down there, but I'm not practicing; I'm not a regular doctor, but a druggist, however, I'll go."[55]

"If he was doped, it was Moran that did it," were the words Turk testified that he said to officer Belcher at the time. Jim Turk then went, himself, to the Portland General Hospital, returning with Drs. Rand and Thomas, who brought with them medical treatment for overdose, including a stomach pump. They applied restoratives, and Dr. Rand injected Kalashua with atropine, but it was of no use. Within a few minutes of their arrival, Kalashua had departed this world, leaving only his muscular frame, grotesquely disjointed by the death throes brought on by morphine and alcohol. Dr. Thomas then stated that it was obvious the man had died of a mixture of alcohol and opiates.[56]

Early the same morning, Dan Moran was arrested on a charge of assault and battery along with the man he was fighting, a man named O'Brien. They were both lodged in the city jail.

The coroner's report stated that Kalashua had been poisoned with alcohol and morphine, and the inquest that followed strongly condemned the actions of Moran, Kelly and the druggist, Dr. Keys, from whom Kelly had obtained the morphine solution. Later on, at trial, officer Belcher would testify that

Kelly, seeing that it would be a short time before his arrest, begged him to arrange it so he could give state's evidence against Moran. Belcher's reply had been, "Kelly, it's too late. Moran has already squealed."

The following evening, James Kelly and Dr. Keys were roused from their beds, placed under arrest and put in the same cell at the jail—a cell with holes created for eavesdropping by detectives. In the adjoining cell, listening to the conversation, was detective Sam Simmons, along with Judge Dement and several police officers. The lawmen stood and listened as Kelly, unaware of his audience, described to the trembling druggist how no one would believe a jailbird like Moran, and how if they stuck together they could put Moran in the hole, and so forth. Kelly was not permitted to see an attorney for several days following his arrest.

The day of the trial came, and the first witness was James Turk, who seemed to not comprehend the seriousness of the matter. After testifying to the manner of his business with the murdered man, Turk tried his hand at a macabre joke:

> He did not receive any portion of the $60, which was advanced to the dead carpenter, because, he said, with a smirk playing all over his glowing face, "I can't ship dead men; I only ship live ones." This observation, which was supposed to be of a humorous nature, did not provoke the change of a facial muscle in the court room [sic].[57]

There was an alternative story afloat that Kelly had doped Kalashua to steal five dollars from him. Mrs. Turk would later testify to that, but on this day she was in such a wretched, hung-over condition that she was deemed useless and excused.

The principal witness, Dan Moran, was then called. Much to the consternation of the members of civil society present in the courtroom, Moran was not forthcoming. The jailer, a man named Dougherty, had allowed the prisoner to escape. Dougherty had set him in an unlocked waiting room, and Moran, dressed in his Sunday best, with a new shine on his boots, had walked out of the jailhouse to freedom.

Dougherty had been at odds with members of the sheriff's department for some time—"open ruction,"[58] it was called in the *Oregonian*. Accusations against Dougherty were many. He had allowed earlier escapes, which were recounted at this time. He was accused of being a friend of Kelly's and interested in sabotaging the trial. A bench warrant was issued for Moran, as were various rewards, including a $200 reward offered by Dougherty himself.

The case against Kelly was convoluted enough that he was eventually acquitted. Dan Moran was captured two weeks later in Spokane Falls and was eventually convicted of first-degree murder. The conviction was appealed, resulting in a new conviction for manslaughter, for which he was sentenced to fifteen years. Oddly enough, it was never pointed out that the only man who would profit by shanghaiing Kalashua back aboard the *Candidate* was Jim Turk. Granted, he "couldn't ship dead men." Or could he?

As horrible as this case was, there is a bright side, of sorts. The legends of the Portland waterfront and shanghaiing often make it sound as if this sort of thing happened nearly daily. The fact that this murder was so shocking and drew so much attention shows that the opposite is true. Drugging unsuspecting victims was a rare thing and, when discovered, drew the wrath of authorities to the fullest extent of the law—usually on some sorry scapegoat.

ANNIE MAGNESS

An equally chilling story from this period can be found between the lines of type in newsprint. It is the story of a young woman who had been a maid in the house of Charles Turk and his wife at 85 North Sixth Street (according to the old address system). On March 19, 1887, Annie Magness appeared in the courtroom of Justice Tuttle to swear out a complaint against Jim and Charles Turk. Interestingly, she was accompanied for moral support by Larry Nevilles, the man the Turks had beaten half to death in James Laidlaw's office years before.

Annie Magness had left the house of Charles Turk, having accepted employment as a domestic with a private family. On the Thursday previous to her appearance in court, she had run into Charles, who had asked her to come with him. The reason for her following Charles was not given, but it is easy for the puritanical mind to jump to conclusions. Charles led the young woman through an alleyway, up a staircase and into an upstairs room, where there was, as the girl put it, "a piano and some gaudy furniture." They entered the room and the girl was surprised to see Jim Turk sitting there. Charles introduced his father and then left the room abruptly, locking the door behind him.[59]

According the Annie Magness's testimony, Jim Turk then proceeded to attempt to rape her. Turk was inebriated and unsteady on his feet. Annie

James Turk's
arrest warrant.
*Author's facsimile
from a photocopy from
the Clatsop County
Historical Society.*

Magness, being young and strong, was able to struggle free and break open the door, making her escape.

Jim Turk was released on a $500 bond while awaiting trial. Charles, who had left the city for Astoria, was arrested by the Clatsop County sheriff and brought back to Portland. Two weeks later, the grand jury returned a "not true" verdict against the men. Annie Magness had failed to show up at the hearing.

This would have been chilling enough in itself had the following not appeared in the *Oregonian* the week after the acquittal:

> *Mrs. L. McClain writes to Justice Tuttle from Clifton, Oregon, asking for information as to the whereabouts of her sister, Annie Magness. The latter had Charles and James Turk arrested for attempt at outrageous assault, and the grand jury ignored the charge. At that time Annie Magness was in charge of Larry Neville, and Mrs. McClain came here in search of her, but didn't find her. She writes that on her return home she has still been industriously inquiring for her sister, but without success, and fears she had* [sic] *met with foul play.*[60]

This was neither the first nor the last instance of the Turks being let off the hook by disappearing witnesses. Not long after this incident, Charles Turk was arrested for allegedly attempting to kidnap and ship a local man named Francis Cassidy. Cassidy swore out a complaint in Justice Bushwiller's court, but when the day came for the hearing, the following headline appeared in the *Oregonian*: "Where's Cassidy."[61]

Chapter 8

THE UNFORTUNATE MR. BEEBY

Many is the tale that begins with some young man setting his face away from the place of his birth to seek his fortune in the wide world. In fairy tales, the young man goes through many tests and trials to triumph in the end. This is not always the way of the world in which you and I live, where many a good man has come to a bad end.

Carroll A. Beeby was born in 1862, the first of six children born to Vernon Taylor Beeby and Sarah Marie Rowe, early pioneers of Houston County, Minnesota. When Carroll Beeby was eleven years old, his mother died in childbirth, and he and one of his sisters were sent to live with an aunt and her family on a farm in Newburg township. According to the family's written and oral history, Beeby was, like many boys in the days of Tom Sawyer and Huckleberry Finn, touched with a bit of wanderlust, running away when he was fifteen years old. He returned, however, and was living with some other relatives at Riceford, Minnesota, when he was about twenty-two years of age.

It was about that time that Beeby decided to go west. Most likely he did so using money he had saved from farm work, buying a ticket on the Northern Pacific to Portland. It was always a thrill for people who lived their lives in the flat reaches of the Midwest to travel through mountains, such as the Rocky Mountains, and through forests that went on, it seemed, for a thousand miles in all directions. It was also a great curiosity to see the ocean, so at Portland, Beeby most likely bought a ticket on the *R.R. Thompson* and steamed down through the beautiful lower Columbia River Valley to Astoria. These were

A young Carroll Beeby before leaving for Oregon. *Cindy Coffin's family archives.*

places he had doubtlessly read about in the magazines of the period, for travel writing was quite popular and did much to bring people west to Oregon. But there was nothing to prepare him for what he would find in Astoria.

It seems like exaggeration to us today—the wholesale wickedness—but if one will bother to look at a detailed Sanborn insurance map of 1880s Astoria, he would find a place with a saloon (listed as "S" or "Sal") and a bawdyhouse (listed as "Ladies res") oftentimes side-by-side with more than several to each block. People often talk about the "hard-working empire builders of the west." They may have worked hard at their various occupations, but a good many of them worked even harder at destroying their souls and bodies with drink and venereal disease, and Astoria was a place where both of these were constantly at one's elbow.

Mr. Beeby was an obvious greenhorn, as I imagine him, in his homespun clothing, carrying a leatherette suitcase. I would suppose he was savvy enough to know this fact, and as a shield against those who prey on such lambs, he looked about the town for a suitable place to lay his head. In Astoria, you can see the wide expanse of the mouth of the Columbia River, but all you can see of the Pacific is a glint in the far distance. Mr. Beeby (again I imagine) would have desired to stand on the beach and see the waves roll down the horizon. After that he would be content to return to the more civilized world of Portland to seek employment.

It is possible he saw a handsome young fellow (like himself), well dressed, with an honest face. He would have stopped such a man and inquired of

Postcard view of Astoria in the snow. *Author's collection.*

him where a good, family boardinghouse might be found. The young man may have turned out to be one of the many sons of Bridget Grant. He would have said, "Dear fellow! You are in luck! My own mother keeps a clean and honest boardinghouse," in which case he would have been led to a pleasant home not far from the business district, with nothing about it to indicate that he was walking headfirst into a life-changing experience.

Mrs. Grant would have been in her early fifties by this time, and if she was described as remarkably handsome ten years earlier, she had at least retained a sparkling charm and sharp wit. Her red hair had taken on the auburn color that age bestows—this combined with the crow's feet about her deep eyes and the lingering blush of fading beauty worked together to make her seem to Beeby even as the mother he had long ago lost.

No doubt Beeby confided in Mrs. Grant many things: the state of his finances and the sort of employment he would seek, and when he spoke of his longing to see the broad Pacific, a knowing smile crept on to the woman's lips, and she said, "We will see what can be arranged." No doubt she saw a wandering young man in search of a vocation—or, more likely, a boy who could be made into a man by a stint on the wild sea.

It is quite probable that there were some old salts about the place, waiting to be shipped. Mrs. Grant never hid the fact from Beeby that her house was primarily for sailors. Then one morning after a solid breakfast, Mrs. Grant asked Mr. Beeby if he could be of help to her, that she was in a difficult predicament. Of course, Mr. Beeby was anxious to help his landlady, whom he now considered to be even a friend. She explained that she had an arrangement with the captain of the *Xenia*, an American bark sitting at anchor in the bay. She was contracted to supply another crew member. Her son, Peter, had secured a man in Portland, who was coming down on the steamboat that evening but not in time for the daily roll call. If the sailor missed roll call, she would be out sixty dollars, the fee she charged to recruit sailors. She didn't want to inconvenience Mr. Beeby, but if he would be so kind as to make the roll call, then the sailor would be there that evening to take his place.

I would imagine that there were some warning bells that rang for Mr. Beeby. It may be that he had become indebted to Mrs. Grant in some way. It may be that some of the old salts who overheard this proposition tapped their pipes on the table or had a fit of coughing, a signal too subtle to be observed.

I can see them in my imagination as they walked together down to the wharf, the elder woman and the lad—Mrs. Grant chatting about the glorious life of a sailor. At the wharf, a long dinghy would be waiting, belonging to the *Xenia*, overseen by a gruff fellow, who would be the vessel's mate. Mrs. Grant would speak to the fellow, and money would be exchanged. Then Beeby would be roughly ushered into the boat. As I imagine it, the last Mrs. Grant saw of the lad was his thin brown hair being pummeled by a stiff breeze from the sea, as the dinghy bobbed and swayed on the currents of the river.

Back in Minnesota, Mr. Beeby's family wondered for many long months what had become of young Carroll. Then a letter came with strange foreign stamps addressed to Carroll Beeby's cousin, Vernon Gilmore:

Barque Elizabeth
Santa Fe, ??[62]
June 20th, 1887.
Dear Sir:
I sit to inform you that your cousin, Carrel Bebby [sic], *was drowned off Cape Horn, from the American Barque,* Xenia, *of Boston, of which Captain Reynolds was master. Your cousin fell from the fore Topgallant yard on the morning of February 12, he being sent up by the second mate to loosen the sail. He missed his hold, fell overboard and was drowned. Dear sir I shipped on board the* Xenia *with your cousin in Astoria, on a voyage*

from there to Bueones Ayres [sic], *S.M. Dear sir your cousin was put on board under false pretences, by Mrs. Grant, who keeps a sailor's boarding house in Astoria, and Portland, Oregon. She asked him if he would go aboard and answer to another man's name. She said she would send the other man aboard that night when he came down from Portland in the steamboat but she never sent him. So I being going to sea for a number of years, I told your cousin what kind of a woman Mrs. Grant was. He had been what us sailors call "shanghied"* [sic] *by her, so he went to the captain and told him his story and said he was no sailor, and he wanted to go ashore again. The captain refused to let him go ashore, saying he had paid Mrs. Grant $60 for him, and that he would have to make the best of it. Dear sir I am very sorry to inform you that your cousin received a great deal of ill treatment from the second mate, John Williams. The night before he was drowned the second mate struck him with a belaying pin on the head, which mark he carried to his grave. The second mate always called him vulgar names which I do not like to mention here. Dear sir, excuse me for not writing to you sooner, but I did not know his father's nor your address. The other day I was looking through my chest and I found your name on a card. I being the only friend he had on board, I kept his papers in my chest. All the papers your cousin had the captain took from me, so I could not write sooner as I had no address 'till I found your name on a card. I*

"Aloft. Jack-tar's Dangerous Work." *Allan C. Green collection of glass negatives, State Library of Victoria, H91.325/2101.*

write you this letter as I am afraid the captain has not informed you of his death. If you want to know any thing about your cousin I will be very glad to tell you what I know.
Yours truly,
Donald McGregor[63]

The tragedy may not have happened exactly as I imagined it, but it was something very much like this. The important thing is that Bridget Grant was rumored to be a shanghaier simply because she and her sons ran sailors' boardinghouses. She was never charged with any crime having to do with shipping sailors, with the exception of one time when she was complicit in hiding a sailor who was required in court as a witness.

This true story of Carroll Beeby is one that offers proof of one of the deceptive ways in which Bridget Grant and other shanghaiers were able to trick, manipulate or cajole weak or unsuspecting men into becoming sailors. It also shows why many "landlubbers" were unable to tell their story. A sailor's work was one of the most dangerous jobs in the world, even for the most skilled and salty jack-tar. An unskilled young man, unaccustomed to climbing ropes in freezing wind and rain, stood a much lesser chance of survival.[64]

Chapter 9

THE ARRIVAL OF JOE "BUNCO" KELLEY

According to records from the Oregon State Penitentiary, Joseph Kelley was born in 1846 in Connecticut.[65] According to Bunco, and nearly everyone else who wrote about him, he was "from Liverpool." It is easy to see how Joseph Kelley (also spelled "Kelly") got the name "Bunco" (also spelled "Bunko"), a nineteenth-century American slang word equivalent to the word "hogwash" today. In those days, a "bunco steerer" was a scam artist. Bunco was a name Kelley had no qualms about using for himself and certainly was one he found easy to live down to.

In 1887, Joseph Kelley appeared on the waterfronts of Portland and Astoria. It is most likely he came here to go into business with his brother, William, who was working as a runner for J.W. Marr's sailors' boardinghouse in Portland. Shortly after his arrival, Bunco Kelley rented a dwelling between C and D Streets on Sixth Street (by the old numbering system),[66] which he used for a short time as a sailors' boardinghouse. This effort failed, and after that, he operated mostly as a runner for other boardinghouses. During this time, the Portland Directory listed all Portland residents, from lowly laborers to exalted judges and bankers. Since Joseph Kelley did not appear in these pages, as did the sailors' boardinghouse keepers and their businesses, it can be safely assumed that he had no permanent residence of his own but shuffled his victims into houses belonging to other crimps or stored them in bawdyhouses or other "low resorts."

In February 1887, the *Daily Astorian* told a story of how the Kelley brothers managed to stir the wrath of Jim Turk and land in court accused of

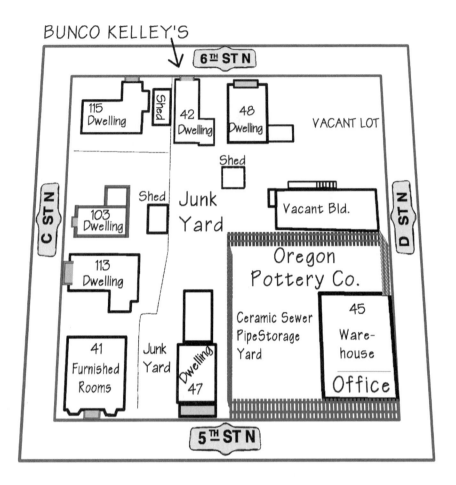

Bunco's first short-lived establishment. *Map by author.*

kidnapping.[67] It appears that the brothers were working for the Turks. Kate was holding down the fort in Portland, and Jim was in Astoria. The Kelley brothers decided to cut Turk out of the deal with two deserting sailors. Mrs. Turk had asked the Kelley brothers to take the men to Astoria aboard the steamboat *Telephone* but instead they kept them hidden away in Portland until they were able to ship them aboard a vessel called the *Arica*.

The *Arica* was cleared by customs in Portland, yet Jim Turk was able to get the men off the ship at Astoria. This meant he had broken a federal law against boarding a vessel once it was cleared. He got the men to his Astoria house, where he proceeded to keep them in a state of alcoholic bliss. Meanwhile the rumor had it the Kelley boys were going to report Turk's action to the authorities. Before they could accomplish this, Turk beat them to the draw by having the two sailors swear out a warrant that the Kelley brothers had kidnapped them. When the kidnapping charge came before a judge, it was seen as obvious retribution, and the Kelley brothers were acquitted. They may have been let off by the courts, but now they had formidable enemies—the Turks.

A month later, the brothers went to work for a used clothing dealer named Arfeld, a man who regularly supplied the other sailors' boardinghouses with clothing for their inmates. Arfeld had decided to try his own hand at "shipping sailors" and had contracted with Sibson, Quackenbush & Co. for $785 to supply sailors for the vessel *County of Flint*, which was to carry a shipment of wheat to Europe. He, in turn, hired Joe and William Kelley to obtain the men he needed, promising them $570 for their effort. When it came time to pay, the money was not forthcoming, and the Kelley brothers took him to court. The case is interesting in that it connects E. Quackenbush, a member of the Seamen's Friend Society, with the process of "shipping sailors," showing that it was an unavoidable part of doing an exporting business on the Pacific Coast.[68]

By April 1887, the name Joe Kelley had become associated with the word "bunco." A ship captain had written a complaint to the *Oregonian* as a warning to other shipmasters to avoid using Kelley's services. He stated, "I was swindled in Portland by 'bunco' Kelly shipping a man aboard my ship, a perfect cripple by rheumatism." Whether he meant to anoint Joe Kelley with a new name or not, hereafter he was known in the press as "Bunco Kelley."[69]

The established sailors' boardinghouse keepers—the Turks, Laura McCormack, Bridget Grant, John Kenney and Larry Sullivan—all tended to work without stepping on one another's toes. Bunco Kelley was always working for himself, even if he was in the hire of another crimp. Since the crimps tended to use the courts as weapons against offending parties, during the nine years he operated as a crimp, Bunco's name appears in court records numerous times, mainly due to warrants sworn against him by his fellow crimps. Taking a friend or even a brother to court was common practice, it seems. Bunco took his brother to court in April 1887 over a fifty-dollar debt and, after his lawsuit against A. Arfeld, still remained in a partnership with him.

By 1890, Joe Kelley had convinced at least one writer at the *Daily Astorian* that he was the "boss shanghaier in the Northwest,[70] who has sent more landsmen to sea than any other man on the coast." He was seen in Astoria as a Portland crimp, and since it was necessary to use Astoria as a final shipping

The vessel *Southesk*. *Brodie Collection, La Trobe Picture Collection, State Library of Victoria, H99.220/1710.*

point to which prospective sailors were brought by steamboat, there was plenty of opportunity for conflict.

The crimps of Portland and Astoria had many bad qualities, but it seems that they had a remarkable ability to not hold on to grudges very tightly. In 1891, harbor policeman John J. Byrne, with the help of constable Al Thomas, arrested a group of crimps trying to entice sailors off the British vessel *Southesk*.[71] They were listed as: "Jim Turk, sailor-boarding-house keeper and Bunco Kelly, sailor boarding-house runner." The other crimps arrested were Paddy Lynch and Dick McCarron. This shows very clearly how the entire entourage was able to work together in "combination," for by this time, McCarron was a member of Sullivan, Grant Bros. & McCarron, and Lynch worked with John Kenney in Astoria. It also shows that even near the end of his career in Portland, Bunco Kelley was considered a "runner," not a "keeper" or "master."

When Kelley was not working directly for a sailors' boardinghouse, he would inter his victims in rented rooms, ones that could lock from the outside. In October 1889, a Samoan sailor complained to the *Oregonian* that Kelley had told him that he kept a sailors' boardinghouse and could get him on a ship. He then proceeded to take him all over the waterfront but was unsuccessful at finding a ship needing a sailor. At eleven that evening, he locked the sailor in an empty room on Second Street near E Street. The Samoan said that he had to pace the floor all night to keep from freezing. The next morning, Kelley opened the door and gave the man fifteen cents to get something to eat.[72]

As late as 1890, Kelley was reported to be the partner of Arfeld. It is possible Arfeld had some rooms that Kelley could use. In 1891, Kelley was arrested and fined for "keeping a disorderly house,"[73] which, according to city ordinance, could mean anything from an unlicensed saloon to a bawdyhouse, but I am inclined to think it was a saloon with "cribs" for prostitutes that could double as bunks for sailors.

In the early 1890s, Kelley had a falling out with Arfeld, who was, after all, only a part-time crimp, trying to make a living selling used clothes. Arfeld then hired his hotheaded brother-in-law, Percy Rosenstein, a two-bit hoodlum who carried a gun he was too afraid to shoot.[74]

Bunco may have claimed the title of "boss shanghaier in the Northwest," but when the ships were stuck in Astoria due to low rivers, he would take his boys down by steamboat—even though trouble often erupted in territory where his authority as "boss" carried no weight. When there were no ships at all, he resorted to bunco schemes, like selling fake opium to the Chinese or rot gut in a blind pig (as unlicensed saloons were called). It is my personal conviction that, had Bunco remained a simple "Joe Kelley," and not stumbled upon a memorable name, had he not been convicted for a vicious murder, he would be no more likely to be remembered than any of the hundreds of other bunco steerers who blew through Portland back when the city was "wide open," when "special policemen" collected monthly fines from all the gambling dens and brothels in the lively Whitechapel.

Chapter 10

BEFORE THE BLIND GODDESS

In 1881, Bridget Grant purchased nine forested acres in the Walluski area on Youngs River, south of Astoria. It came to be rumored that Mrs. Grant was able to get rid of the trees and turn this land into a viable farm by using deserting sailors who were hiding out until the heat was off. It was also rumored that the laborers on this little plantation did so under the careful eyes of armed guards. But these were mere rumors. Unlike all the other people connected with the sailors' boardinghouses of Astoria, Bridget was rarely made to stand before the stern gaze of a judge—until, that is, she spirited away the wrong sailor at the wrong time.

Early in 1889, the American bark *C.S. Hulbert* was in route to the Columbia River. On board was the usual collection of tars, but one of them, a man named Richard Jewel, was not as experienced as the others. This gave rise to some incidents between Jewel and the first mate, a burly chap named Davis. It seems that Jewel couldn't be left at the wheel without steering off course. He was also not much at listening to orders, using the wrong rope on sails and other irritating offences. When Jewel spilled paint all over some sails, Davis lost his cool and cuffed the man, knocking him down.

Once in Portland, Jewel was discovered by one of the many shyster lawyers who combed the waterfront dives looking for reasons to libel a ship. Hearing Jewel's story, exaggerated by libations, a warrant was drawn up for the arrest of Davis. However, Richard Jewel and one of the other sailors, a man named John Ding, were suddenly removed from

Portland, having been invited by a sailors' boardinghouse runner to take a trip on the *R.R. Thompson* to Astoria and the comfortable quarters of Mrs. Grant. When Jewel's case came before U.S. Circuit Court judge Deady, neither Richard Jewel nor the three other witnesses from the ship could be found. U.S. marshals were dispatched to round up the witnesses. They found two of the sailors in some waterfront dives, but Jewel and Ding were still missing.

Fleet of foot, Larry Sullivan high-tailed it down to Astoria and, according to Jewel's later testimony, burst into Mrs. Grant's with the news: "Get Dick out of the way! They are coming after him!" U.S. marshal Roberts was savvy enough about such things to be able to trace the steps of the crimps as far as Astoria. The Clatsop County sheriff balked for a while, unwilling to let Roberts discover Mrs. Grant's rural hideaway. Eventually, Roberts was placated with the sheriff's promise that he would deliver them into his hands before the next steamboat left for Portland. As good as his word, he returned with everyone listed on the warrant before the final whistle. The roster included Richard Jewel, John Ding, Larry Sullivan, Bridget Grant, Laura McCormick, Peter Grant and John Grant.[75]

The steamboat journey must have been an odd spectacle for those who knew what was going on. Most likely Marshal Roberts, the sailors, Larry Sullivan and the Grant boys all played cards and joked together. Mrs. McCormick would have spent a great deal of her time trying to make sure Bridget Grant was comfortable. Bridget, on the other hand, was mostly silent and furious. The others may have thought that being hauled into court was a part of doing business, but for her, it was not.

In the seemingly inexplicable hot and cold periods of laws being enforced against the crimps, the year 1889 is a particularly hot one, most likely due to the political climate. Judge Mathew Deady must have been more than a little irritating to the accused, peering over his spectacles and "tut-tutting" as though he had never seen such a thing in all his life. He dismissed them with a "remove them from my sight" wave of his hand and a stiff $750 in bonds. When they appeared for the trial a few weeks later, his tune had modified. John Grant proved his innocence and was found not guilty. The rest of the defendants were found guilty but fined a mere $50 each, which they were happy to shell out on the spot. Judge Deady offered this insight as an excuse for his lenience: had they been found guilty by a jury, he would have been compelled to send them to prison. But since he had acted as both judge and jury, "he felt a

A typical Pacific Northwest saloon. *A.M. Kendrick Photographic Collection, Washington State Archives, 008-0807.*

Postcard view of Portland grain warehouses and dock. *Author's collection.*

delicacy in subjecting them to the full penalty of the law for fear he might be mistaken."

The crimps had been caught red-handed. It is difficult to see how the judge could fear he might be mistaken. If there was any indication that Deady had been the recipient of graft, the decision might make more sense—but such evidence is not known.

Chapter II

EVENTS LEADING UP TO THE FUNERAL OF JAMES TURK

LORD CANNING

The autumn of 1889 was a nasty period for James Turk. As he had done a hundred times before, he sailed out from the Astoria dock in his dinghy and climbed the Jacob's ladder of a newly arrived British bark, *Lord Canning*. Once aboard, he successfully persuaded a number of crew members to enjoy the amenities of his sailors' hotel, complete with such beverages and other pleasures that had been denied them these many long months at sea.

In the complex world of international business, it had been decided—behind Turk's back—that the days of the usefulness of crimps and the sailors' boardinghouse system were over. The Portland office of the charterers of the *Lord Canning*, the powerful British commodities merchants, Balfour, Guthrie & Co., had notified the ship's master, Thomas Stevenson, that to everyone's profit (except Turk's) they would prosecute Turk to establish a precedent (if possible) for enforcing the existing laws against the desertion of sailors, advanced wages and all the other nefarious details of the business. The attorneys for the charterers furthermore requested that the Portland Board of Trade take up proceedings against Turk, using the *Lord Canning* incident as a test case.[76] Following procedure, the charterer's attorneys first sent Turk a letter demanding the immediate return of the sailors, then they brought charges, with the assurance that the Portland business community gave them their full support.

Portland Harbor. *City of Portland, Oregon archives, A2004-002.341.*

On September 15, 1889, Turk was arrested in Astoria and brought to Portland, where he was released on a bond of $1,000. As Turk and his wife owned large amounts of property in both cities, there was no fear that he would fail to appear. The arraignment was set before Judge Stearns in the criminal court for September 20, 1889, but when the day arrived, James Turk did not. In his stead, a rather rumpled-looking junior solicitor appeared, out of breath from his hurried trek to the courthouse from the steamboat dock. He brought with him an affidavit from D.F. Winton, Turk's attorney, stating that Mr. Turk was unfit to travel. It read, "Will you kindly consent to let him remain here for say ten days so that he will not be anxious about being compelled to go to court? The doctor says that he should be kept free from all excitement for some days to come. Turk is on the verge of delirium tremens."[77]

To everyone's surprise, Jim Turk showed the next day on schedule, alongside the rest of the criminal lineup before Judge Stearns. He did not look like he was ill; in fact, he was described by a reporter as "most conspicuous by reason of his extensive corporosity…Jim was as rosy-cheeked and burly and lumbersome as ever. He did not look as if he had recently been under treatment for delirium tremens."

94

The trial went forward the same day as the arraignment, before Judge Tanner in the state criminal court against Jim Turk, "Astoria sailor's boardinghouse keeper."[78] The prosecution centered its case on a single deserting seaman, a J. Walmer, whom Turk was accused of harboring. The captain of the *Lord Canning* had set aside his sailing date so that his chief mate, George Moore, could testify. Moore told how Turk had boarded the vessel illegally and had set about enticing members of his crew to desert. What he did not mention was that this scenario had been repeated every time a vessel came into port for as long as anyone could remember. In his defense, Turk said he had never laid eyes on J. Walmer.

The jury was out for twenty-four hours and forty-five minutes before resigning to the fact that there were four men who would never vote to convict. They were hung. The *Oregonian* quipped that a jury made up of blind men with cotton stuffed in their ears would have convicted him, insinuating a lack of community spirit to the four belligerent members.

With insult swiftly following on the heels of misery, James Turk received an official summons to appear the very next evening at a meeting of the Portland Board of Trade, a group made up of all of Portland's highbrow businessmen. They made it clear that failure to appear would affect his ability to do business in Portland. The president was the old Scottish-born Portland merchant Donald Macleay, who had been in business with H.W. Corbett since 1866. This firm, along with John McCracken, was the first exporters of wheat directly from Portland to England, cutting San Francisco out of the deal. The rest of the members of the board read like a who's who of old Portland capitalists, bankers and merchants of the sort James Turk would have loved to have sat among—on their walnut armchairs, upholstered in green leather, in their carriages, with their houses on Nob Hill.

I imagine that before heading over to the board of trade meeting, Turk, no doubt, stopped at a saloon for something to steady his nerves, and by the time he left, he felt better but had become slightly unsteady on his feet. By the standards of today's traffic policeman, he was drunk.[79] As he climbed the steps to the meeting rooms at the New Market Theater building, Turk must have felt like some besmirched shepherd straying on Mount Olympus. The meeting was already underway, and instead of a cordial acknowledgement of his deigning to appear, he was made to stand in the hallway while an attendant notified Mr. Donald Macleay of his presence.

Mr. Macleay excused himself for a moment and went to the hallway to bring Jim Turk in and see him seated until it was time for his case to be presented. Disapproving looks may or may not have been cast Turk's

The New Market Theater. *From* The West Shore *(1879).*

direction, but at his level of mental instability, it must have seemed to him as though he had entered before the judgment seat of the gods. To make matters even worse, the room was filled to overflowing with members. They were not primarily there to see him. The main issue advertised in the papers was the fact that the U.S. Navy was looking to build a dry dock on the north Pacific Coast, and Portland needed to act.[80]

After an extended period of stern discussion on the topic of "shipping sailors," Donald Macleay invited Mr. Turk to address the chamber.[81] Turk was at a low point. His head was still spinning from having been bushwhacked

for something he had done so many times that it was as natural as getting out of bed. The acoustics of the room in which the chamber met were notoriously bad, and Turk was unaccustomed to public speaking. He was also unaccustomed to being outnumbered by strong-minded men. The preponderance of ill will had brought up many mixed feelings in this man who, as any man, wanted acceptance. An unaccustomed feeling was welling up within him, one of guilt. Adding to this guilt, the alcohol in his blood addled within him a surge of self-pity. Burdened down with all this, Jim Turk began to address the chamber in a croak, fighting back tears.

He told how he and his little family had come to Portland just as the first sailors had started to arrive. He saw that someone needed to take care of them during the time they had in port. He told how he had never turned away a man who applied to him for lodging in his life. He took in the poor jack-tars and the downtrodden vagrant. All he asked was an honest return for his efforts. Then in recent years, he had seen the rise of such men as the Grant boys and Larry Sullivan combination and runners like Paddy Lynch and Bunco Kelley—greedy, bad men. Instead of standing his ground, he had become bad himself to stay alive. The Astoria combination had threatened his very life if he didn't throw in with them.

He said he had made up his mind to leave Astoria and the bad men there. He would move back to Portland and ship sailors at the lawful rates. He was further reported to have told the astonished board members, "They don't carry on right, and I don't do right myself. I am willing to do right and take no more than the Board of Trade allows for sailors."

He said he would go down to Astoria and see that the *Lord Canning* got a crew. He would sell his house at Astoria and quit the combinations there, not because of the trouble he was in. He hoped that matter would be overlooked and there would be no more of it. He promised faithfully to obey the law and to study the interests of the commerce of Portland.[82]

He had spoken as if he were a repentant sinner testifying at a tent revival. Who could challenge such newfound sincerity? There was a ripple of hesitant applause, and Citizen Turk left the room flushed. Then the men turned their thoughts to weightier matters.

True to his word, Citizen Turk boarded the *R.R. Thompson* for passage to Astoria. He began selling off his property, although by this time, Catherine would hear none of it. She had her own property, under her own name, Catherine Murray. Not missing a beat, the *Daily Morning Astorian* published a piece called "Jim Turk Leaves Astoria Again, Will Not Come Back Anymore (Maybe)":

> "*I've left Astoria for good and I'm going to stay in town where I shall furnish crews to ship captains at the regular rate allowed by law, which is $40 advance money and $10 for shipping. I wanted to inaugurate that scheme at Astoria, but the boys threatened to take my life. They were getting $87.50 a head for every man shipped, and a reduction of $37.50 would make quite a difference.*"
>
> "*You don't mean that you were afraid of being murdered?*" asked an Astorian reporter?
>
> "*Indeed I was. I am not as young and spry as I was, and don't want to take any desperate chances. I'll never go back to Astoria, I want to dispose of all my property there even if I have to do it at a sacrifice.*"[83]

Albina grain docks and Portland Harbor. Photographer unknown. *Author's collection.*

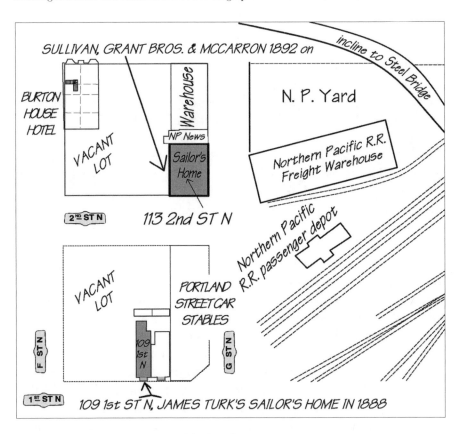

North End sailors' boardinghouses. *Map by author.*

Citizen Turk was informed he would be tried again in criminal court, this time for harboring a deserter. The trial on October 15 resulted in a swift acquittal, with a majority of the jurors in agreement. Undeterred, Quackenbush, E.M. Deady and the U.S. district attorney went to work on bringing the case before a federal judge. A week later, federal judge Lorenzo Sawyer issued a bench warrant for J. Walmer, one of the deserters from the *Lord Canning*, to be held as a witness. Walmer foolishly resisted arrest and ended in the county jail with bruises all over his face. The injuries didn't come from the arrest though, but from Citizen Turk, who had discovered the man was trying to ship out on the *Cambrian Queen* without the aid of a boarding master. When Turk heard this, he became enraged and beat Walmer with a nearby log of firewood.

On December 15, Turk was convicted for similar charges arising from the same incident in Judge Deady's court. The whole affair was brought to an end with a fine of $100.

SOME INSCRUTABLE MISTAKE OF DIVINE PROVIDENCE

Sometime before this, Turk's wife, now living in Astoria, had reached a state of dissipation close to the point of insanity. She had always helped to make his life either a taste of hell or a wee bit of heaven. She hated and resented Turk's son Charles but had doted on the little rascal of hers, Frank, his entire life. The problems with Charles had been so bad that recently she had sworn out a warrant against him, claiming that he had tried to kill her with a "deadly weapon."[84] She had also gone on a rampage, busting shop windows and ending in jail.[85]

On a visit to Portland, Mrs. Turk and her little darling, Frank, had assaulted Joe "Bunco" Kelley on a city street in broad daylight, threatening to kill him. Frank was by this time a hefty post-pubescent, and it looked to the skinny-armed Bunco—big on mouth, small on brawn—as though the lad could actually make good the threat. Bunco swore out a warrant, and once again, the courts were forced to intervene.

Turk was selling out of his Astoria property, spending more time focused on business other than sailors. It was clear to Jim Turk, even if no one else noticed, that Kate was no longer merely an obnoxious drunk but rather that her brain had been eaten away by alcohol and that she was unaware of her actions after extended blackouts. In this case, tragedy was bound to occur.

The tragedy came by what the *Astorian* called "some inscrutable mistake of Divine Providence." Somehow, a little girl had been left in the care of Catherine Turk. It was most likely the work of a prostitute who felt she could no longer provide for the little child. Mrs. Turk had probably cooed over the girl, and the prostitute, knowing that money was never a problem for Mrs. Turk, had either sold or given the child over to her care.[86]

Soon after this, the child's cries of pain brought a visit by a Mr. Beasley, an Astoria town constable, who upon seeing the child's wounds, immediately removed her from Mrs. Turk. The child was taken to Saint Mary's Hospital, and Mrs. Turk was taken to jail, under arrest for bringing grievous bodily harm to a child. When the matter was brought before Justice Cleveland in police court a day or so later, Mrs. Turk was fined fifty dollars plus court costs—a judgment that seemed to be the standard penalty for heinous crimes that would bring stiff sentences today. On the same day as this judgment, Jim Turk was arraigned before the same judge for mercilessly beating an old man, known to all as "old man McIntyre."

This was the last public humiliation of this troubled woman. In mid-January 1890, she died of what the *Astorian* called *"la grippe."*[87] This was the common way of identifying Spanish influenza but was also used for nearly every other sickness not known to doctors. Kate took her final steamboat passage to Portland, and was laid to rest in the frozen ground of the Lone

Postcard of St. Mary's hospital, where Kate Turk died. *Author's collection.*

Fir Cemetery, in the plot next to Jim Turk's mother. Her husband ordered that there be erected a fine granite monument, inscribed with the touching words: "Catherine Murray, beloved wife of James Turk, died January 14, 1890, Age 47 Yrs, 9 Ms, 7 Ds. After a mourning period of six weeks, Turk married again, a woman named Elizabeth M. Gardner, of whom almost nothing is known.

SLABTOWN HOTEL AND DEATH

Apparently Jim Turk did not sell out of Astoria fast enough. In March, he was skewered by the *Oregonian* as an "Astoria boarding master" and a "pirate" well loved in Astoria for the money he brought into the local coffers stolen from honest sailors. This was just a few weeks after the *Astorian* had declared him to be a Portland shanghaier who "stands by Portland, and Portland stands by him."[88] It is hard to follow any reason for this, unless it was all a smoke screen to keep the heat away from the rapidly developing business of Sullivan, Grant Bros. & McCarron, now firmly established in Portland. There is a possibility that they were part of a "combination" in collusion to extract

the highest possible fees from ships. When Jim Turk left Portland for a short while in January 1891, to see if the grass was greener in Tacoma, the *Oregonian* reported as much in an article called "A Combination Broken Up."[89]

While the old man was away, young Frank tried to walk in his shoes. In March, Jim had to return to Portland to get his son out of a jam. He had been arrested with two of his hoodlum buddies for trying to entice sailors off of a ship, something severely frowned upon (unless you were connected with Larry Sullivan). Jim pleaded that the boy was celebrating his twentieth birthday. They wouldn't put a boy in jail on his birthday, would they? They said that they would and fined him a hefty $300, which his father paid. The other two boys, the court figured, were just being used by Frank and were fined $30 each. Having no money meant thirty days in the jailhouse or worse—the rock pile. It appears that Turk stayed in town for a while after this to keep tabs on the boy.

Turk, however, wasn't as spry as he once was. The reports of drunken assaults and altercations by the old man became fewer, as those of both

View of the Portland Lumber Company and Slabtown. *City of Portland, Oregon archives, A2004-002.7767.*

sons increased. During this period, Turk started to operate out of a hotel he had purchased years earlier. The place was located at 350 Fourteenth North (by the old address system), one block from Campbell's Ballast Dock. This was true "Slabtown." The hotel is shown on the detailed Sanbourn Map of the period as being surrounded on three sides by "piles of wood slabs." This was another house with an identity crisis, at first being called the "Garfield Hotel" and then the "Hoffman House," before reverting to its original name. During a period of Jim Turk's absence, the new Mrs. Turk tried christening the establishment "The American Exchange Hotel," but this effort was short-lived.

A hotel surrounded by woodpiles next to a ballast dock was not the sort of place to draw high-class clients. Before long, Citizen Turk was filling the rooms with old salts and wandering hoboes—men who considered a life at sea as slightly better than a life at the rock pile. Once, though, when the ships were scarce and sailors were plentiful, Turk found himself stuck with a hotel full of deadbeats. When Frank asked some of them to cut firewood, they refused. Maybe it was the tone in Frank's voice that rankled them. The upshot was that Frank told his daddy, and Jim Turk threw them out. It was reported in the *Oregonian* under the heading: "Turk and His Sailors—The Jolly Tars Refuse to Saw Wood and Quit Their Boarding-house."[90] Turk said he was lodging and feeding twenty-five men at that time and some had been there for seven weeks. He threw them out but kept their clothes and other belongings to pay for the services provided.

Shortly after this, Portland and Astoria were treated to a surprise, and one that proved how wrong Mr. Quackenbush had been in his assessment of John Byrne as harbor policeman. Thirteen members of the crew of the barkentine *Southesk* deserted into the Portland night. They were hidden from view in a nearby sailors' boardinghouse until it was time for the night boat to Astoria. Just as they were about to embark, their game was foiled by Officer Byrne and several constables from the criminal court. The perpetrators in this affair turned out to be Jim Turk, Bunco Kelley, Paddy Lynch and Dick McCarron, giving credence again to the whole "combination" idea. Turk and Kelley were arrested immediately, whereas McCarron and Lynch escaped. McCarron was picked up in Astoria the next day, while Lynch managed to go on the lam.

A week or so later, Turk was arrested for threatening to kill a sailor, but the sailor failed to appear at the hearing. It was getting to be like old times. In an article called "Pests of the Port,"[91] the trials of all the men arrested, including an added arrest of Larry Sullivan, came to naught in a trial before

Looking down on the Boss Saloon and Burnside Bridge at Northwest Flanders and Front Streets. *City of Portland, Oregon archives, A2004-002.6815.*

Judge Deady. By mutual agreement, the jury was dispensed with, and the verdict was "not guilty" (again, one supposes, by mutual agreement). It is almost comical to see the build-up of the story, starting with the quick police work of Officer Byrne and ending in an unremarked-upon hush surrounding the acquittal.

Jim Turk did not exit the business as he had promised. Instead, he broadened his scope. By 1894, not only was he running up and down the Columbia between Portland and Astoria by steamboat, but he was also moving across the Columbia on the Northern Pacific ferry at Kalama and on to Tacoma by rail. It isn't known whether he was intending to move to Tacoma or whether he had set the business up for his son Charles. Catherine Turk had left her darling Frank what was then a significant fortune of $20,000, but she had left nothing for Charles. Frank was intent on filling his father's shoes, with the help of his hoodlum friends, in Portland and Astoria. It is only reasonable that Tacoma was meant for Charles. The world was ripe for the picking for such men. Jim Turk considered that he must become stronger, not weaker, as some supposed he had.

The year 1894 was ushered in with the *Oregonian* reporting, yet again, the "combination" of boarding masters was dissolved, with Jim Turk removing himself to "branch out in his own line."[92] It must have made Jim Turk a bit nervous to be in business with uncouth and unskilled hoodlums like his son Frank and Paddy Lynch. They had no skill in legal matters, setting up witnesses and such. Besides this, they had no concept of propriety. They even lowered themselves to assault women, such as Maggie Gurrey, who kept a saloon on Couch Street.

Frank, left in charge of his father's boardinghouse, began to get the attention once reserved for his father. Not content to fill his father's shoes, the lad had the extra ambition to try and fill the shoes of the prizefighter Larry Sullivan as well. In April, he was arrested for his first in a series of arrests for participating in illegal prizefights. These were gladiatorial, bare-knuckles affairs in which it was rumored men even sometimes fought to the death.

JIM TURK EXPIRES

This was a time when "Tammanyizing" of the city government and police force was well under way, with graft and vice seeping in at all the cracks. A "Committee of One Hundred Taxpayers" was formed from members of the business community concerned that the city was going to hell in a handbasket. H.W. Corbett, the old senator and grain merchant, was president. The committee met in November 1894 to discuss the decay. The city tax collector, a man named Abe Tichenor, was said to be one of the largest owners of property in Whitechapel and owned several large houses of prostitution himself. Mayor Frank had caved in to the shanghaiers and had removed John Byrne as harbor policeman, filling the position with a nice but weak fellow of Larry Sullivan's choosing. Gambling houses were under police protection, being charged fees to make up the salaries of "special policeman." It was mentioned by Mr. Goldsmith, a former mayor and early Portland settler, that Jim Turk had cost the city $50,000 over the past years in the prosecution of criminal charges and assault and battery cases. "Still he is more powerful than the Committee of One Hundred. It must be that he provides repeaters on election day." There was a war coming. The *Oregonian* called it a "War on Gamblers,"[93] but it was a war against the stench of evil and moral decay that permeated the North End and bulged the bank accounts of those whose duty it was to uphold the standards of society.

While Mr. Goldsmith spoke those words, calling Jim Turk "more powerful than the Committee of One Hundred," Jim Turk was in Tacoma, at his

Northern Pacific Railroad ferry *Tacoma* arriving during a flood that prevented its normal crossing from Kalama to Hunters (Goble). *City of Portland, Oregon archives, A2004-002.692.*

son Charles's boardinghouse. His lack of spryness had rapidly deteriorated into ghastly illness—an illness that never lifted. On January 5, 1895, he breathed his last. Having been gone from Portland for a month or so, his obituary in the *Oregonian*[94] made it sound as though he had long ago moved his operations to Tacoma. As far as the paper was concerned, he was now a "Tacoma sailor's boardinghouse master."

He was buried between his mother and his beloved Kate in the frozen ground of the Lone Fir Cemetery. The funeral was attended by every boarding master, crimp and runner from Astoria to Portland.

Chapter 12

A CONFEDERACY OF CRIMPS

Rivals

By the late 1880s, the crimps had made themselves odious enough that the state legislature was discussing adding its own laws to those already in place at a federal level. It may have been the paranoid rant of an Astoria newspaper editor, but in an anonymous article in the *Daily Astorian* in 1888, the Portland business community was accused of strong-arming the Oregon legislature into obeying its every whim. The article purported the following:

> [The Astorian] *was informed yesterday that a prominent shipping merchant of Portland made a proposition to two Astoria sailor boarding house proprietors in his office in Portland that if they would move their business from* "that place" [Astoria] "up here," [Portland] *that he would* "see that the sailor boarding house bill was killed in the legislature.*

This was another in the continual nagging of the Astoria press that Portland was always out to undercut the "New York of the Pacific" at the mouth of the Columbia. According to the *Daily Astorian*, if a sailors' boardinghouse was in Portland, sharing the wealth with the authorities there, it could do no wrong, in the eyes of the Portland authorities, but if it was centered in Astoria, the boardinghouse masters were "pirates, robbers, unblushing scoundrels, and so on."

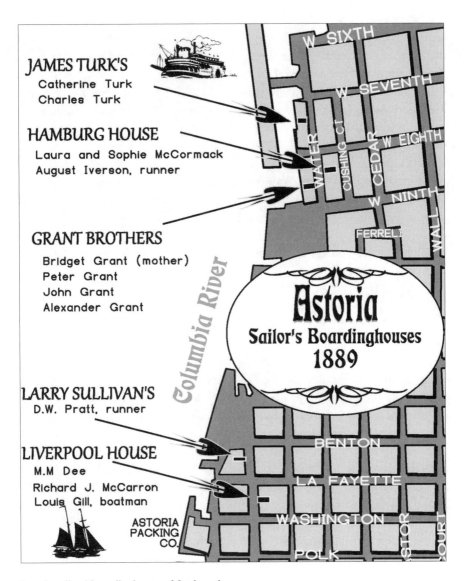

JAMES TURK'S
Catherine Turk
Charles Turk

HAMBURG HOUSE
Laura and Sophie McCormack
August Iverson, runner

GRANT BROTHERS
Bridget Grant (mother)
Peter Grant
John Grant
Alexander Grant

Astoria
Sailor's Boardinghouses
1889

LARRY SULLIVAN'S
D.W. Pratt, runner

LIVERPOOL HOUSE
M.M Dee
Richard J. McCarron
Louis Gill, boatman

ASTORIA PACKING CO.

Astoria sailors' boardinghouses. *Map by author.*

This rumor must have reached the ears of the members of the firm Sullivan, Grant Bros. & McCarron. In 1891, while the Grants continued operations in Astoria, Sullivan and McCarron moved to a building near Portland's waterfront. It was the old Wilson House, a respectable, North End hotel located at 113 North Second Street, not far from Jim Turk's old place. By this time, Turk had moved to the Garfield Hotel in Slabtown. In

1894, the Grant brothers—Peter, Jack and, intermittently, Alex—moved to the Portland location as well. The grip Jim Turk once held was weakening. By spreading out to Tacoma, Turk had loosened his grip in Portland. Besides this, leaving his Portland business in the hands of two hoodlums like Frank Turk and Paddy Lynch shows that his faculties of judgment were failing.

When Jim Turk began to falter, there was a period of several years where bumbling amateurs seemed to crop up from nowhere. The violence arising from this period added fuel to the fire beneath the feet of Oregon legislators to do something. In Astoria gangs of young men, unemployed school chums of some of the boardinghouse keepers, added their strength to the threats against ship masters and rival boardinghouses. It was a game in which the most ruthless were winners, and since Larry Sullivan, the Grant brothers and John McCarron came out on top, one can assume that they are behind some of the more disturbing reports of violence.

Violence between boarding masters reached a peak early in 1889.[95] In January of that year, Captain Carlson, of the Norwegian bark *Jerusalem*, complained to the Norwegian consul of the violence his ship was subjected to during a period in which the ship was at the Astoria anchorage. While he was away on business in Portland, with his wife, two children and the entire crew left on board, twelve men climbed onto the ship and began to try to forcibly remove the men. They tore the clothes off some men and, armed with jugs of whiskey, began pouring whiskey down sailors' throats. One man was tied hand and foot as whiskey was poured down his throat. When the captain's wife came out of her cabin and demanded that the men leave, "all of them, armed with pistols and knives, abused her with foul language, threatening her life." Eventually they left, taking four members of the crew with them. The authorities at Astoria obviously were not interested in these abuses, and the U.S. marshals were greatly outnumbered. In this environment, the "pirates of the port" felt that they were beyond the reach of the law.

The Portland courts had shown themselves, over the years, to be rather kind to Jim Turk, and recently they had given the same deference to Sullivan and McCarron. In 1890, even before moving to Portland, a $10,000 lawsuit by a young German man, who had been shipped by Sullivan and McCarron with just the clothes on his back, was thrown out because he had signed the ship's articles willfully. He had been offered $30 to sign and $50 advance money, from which he was told he could purchase supplies for the trip but ended up with nothing. He suffered without blankets, tobacco, oilskins, personal hygiene articles or even a change of clothes, for a long voyage, which was extended by two months due to bad weather.

During this period of transition, Larry Sullivan was often in the news for fighting in (and out) of the ring and for illegalities involved in the shipping of sailors. In the ring, he was usually beaten, as when he lost to Portland's favorite, Dave Campbell, in a well-publicized bout in 1900. Outside the ring, he was usually the aggressor and always came out on top, even when his opponent was a member of the law enforcement community.

In 1891, Larry Sullivan and Bunco Kelley began working together, a partnership that covered both ports. In October, they were both arrested for enticing sailors to desert and for stealing the same sailors' belongings. By now, the standard punishment for crimes related to crimping was a $100 fine, which became an occasional setback, a part of the cost of doing business.

THE *HARVEST QUEEN* INCIDENT

From one incident that happened in July 1892, a very clear picture can be drawn of the confederacy of crimps (called a "combination" by the press) that was coming together. Paddy Lynch, who had taken over the old Turk place on C Street, was bringing four drunken stragglers of a ten-man crew to Astoria aboard the steamboat *Harvest Queen*. The other six men were already aboard the British ship *Grandee*, at anchor in the Astoria harbor. When the steamboat stopped at Cathlamet to "wood up," much to Lynch's dismay, the vessel was boarded by Larry Sullivan, Bunco Kelley and Peter Grant. Naturally, Lynch was verbally abused, and equally naturally, he was unable to keep his mouth shut, going so far as to purposely allow his revolver to be seen in a shoulder holster as an unspoken threat. An enraged Sullivan then took the revolver away from Lynch and beat him severely. When the steamboat arrived in Astoria, Lynch and his drunken victims stayed aboard the steamboat, waiting for a launch to take them to the *Grandee*. Meanwhile, Sullivan and his friends saw that a rumor reached the ear of U.S. deputy marshal Stuart that Lynch had shanghaied some sailors.[96]

Deputy Marshal Stuart took charge of the situation. He took a launch to the *Grandee* and found that two of the men were so drunk they were unable to say whether or not they had signed the ship's articles willingly. Stuart had them arrested for their own protection and took them ashore. The captain of the *Grandee*, anxious to avoid trouble and get to sea, shipped a crew from Sullivan, Grant Bros. & McCarron and sent Lynch's crew packing. Lynch immediately telegraphed Judge Deady in Portland asking that the ship be

"Wooding up." Steamboats used an enormous amount of cordwood to operate. *From* The West Shore *(1888)*.

libeled[97] for the money owed to him for providing the men. By this time, the two sailors in the drunk tank were sober enough to let everyone know that they had indeed shipped willingly. Insult was then added to Lynch's injuries. The Sullivan boys swore out a warrant for Lynch's arrest for attempting to assault them with his revolver, and he was hauled off to the Astoria jail.

These flare-ups between crimps clogged up the jails and the courts, but the law was the law, even if it was merely used as a weapon between rival shanghaiers. Later in that year, while Larry Sullivan and Dick McCarron were in Portland looking for a place to relocate, Sullivan became embroiled in a fierce fistfight with harbor policeman John Byrne. Sullivan, covered with mud and howling that he had lost a $350 ring somewhere during the fray, was dragged into court by several policemen. His opponent had been beaten so severely he couldn't talk. The story Sullivan was telling the police court appeared to be leading to a trial that, according to the news report, promised to reveal some inside facts of the crimping business. Sullivan was complaining that Byrne had tried to arrest him on some trumped-up charge in an attempt to force him into renting some property he owned on the waterfront that he claimed was suitable for a boardinghouse. This had happened, he continued, even though he had an agreement to pay Byrne $250 per month. Sullivan further claimed that, during their argument, Byrne had suddenly punched him in the head and started to choke him—a story that seems unlikely, due to Sullivan's reputation.

Sullivan was lodged in the city jail and given a bond of $800, which was soon paid by a chatty and magnanimous Bunco Kelley. Kelley (who was incorrectly identified as "John Kelly" in the article) told the wide-eyed reporter that he was "now on the top of the heap" and would just as gladly pay $8,000 bail for his friend as $800, even though the "combination" had him thrown in jail once. He went on to describe how he had been insulted by the jailer as he was paying Sullivan's bonds and ended his little speech with the information that there wasn't a man on earth he owed twenty-five cents nor that could say he had done them wrong. Since Bunco was working for Sullivan at the time, it is almost certain the money was Sullivan's to begin with.[98]

All those interested in the "inside facts" that were to be revealed in the upcoming trial were sorely disappointed. His lawyers argued that Sullivan had been cleared of the charges earlier, in the police court, and could not be tried a second time for the same trial. As confusing as this might be to us today, it worked, and Sullivan was released.

The new Sailor's Home at 113 North Second Street was a hotel next to the Northern Pacific Rail yard, not far from where Couch Lake had been filled in and the new Union Station was being built. It wasn't the Ritz, but it wasn't a flophouse either. It would serve as the new Sailor's Home for years to come. Sullivan, Grant Bros. & McCarron were no longer identified in the press as being "Astoria sailor's boardinghouse" crimps, the appellation now being "North End." To begin with, the members of the firm boarded at the new facility in Portland, as can be seen by their entries in the Portland Directory—including Joseph (Bunco) Kelley, who is listed as "clerk" of the firm. Kelley was unpredictable, disloyal and greedy—Sullivan doubtlessly thought he needed a short leash.

Sullivan, Grant Bros. & McCarron came to town with bags of money saved from Astoria crimping. Soon after their arrival, a fair amount of this money was put to the use of greasing the gears of the well-known "Portland Machine," as the ruling Republican Party was called. The nabobs of the party believed in "free enterprise" when it came to gambling, alcohol and prostitution. Some of them even owned North End properties where such vice was practiced. There was another faction of the party that was in favor of stamping out vice, so it seemed a good idea to invest in keeping those reformers from getting the upper hand.

In Portland, the firm set about using the services of J.P. Betts as a "shipping master" to represent the firm to the ship captains. Betts—once a ship captain and stevedore in Astoria—was by then a part of the highest levels of the "Portland Machine" and a member of the Masonic "Mystic Shrine" to boot. With their newfound political base, Sullivan and his associates were in business like never before.

JOE KELLEY, THE JAILBIRD

Having Bunco Kelley as an employee was an effort that was bound to fail. By September 1894, Bunco had broken away from the firm, setting up in business with George Powers, an old acquaintance from Astoria who was well known to the police. Together they rented a flophouse to use as a sailors' boardinghouse on B Street. Bunco's departure was not treated amenably by Sullivan's group, with threats and hostilities growing until Sullivan and McCarron happened upon Bunco and Powers on the corner of Second and Ankeny, culminating into what the news report described as "A Lively Street Fight." The four gentlemen were taken to jail, with Bunco and Powers filing an assault charge against the other two men. They were all charged with disturbing the peace. Three days later, all these peccadilloes would seem very minor to Bunco Kelley—for that day, October 6, 1894, a headline on the tenth page of the *Oregonian* declared the gruesome tragedy:

> *Old Man Slain*
> *G.W. Sayres Hacked to Death with his Body Thrown in River.*
> *"Bunco" Kelly, "Bob" Garthorne and Four Others in Custody—the Motive a Mystery.*

Much has been written about this murder, the most extensive treatment being found in J.D. Chandler's *Murder and Mayhem in Portland, Oregon*, and many theories arose over the motivation and the guilty party or parties. Bunco declared himself to be victim of a plot by Larry Sullivan to get him out of the way. This was never shown to be the case, but nonetheless, he was conveniently put out of the picture, just at a time when he could prove to be most troublesome to the "combination." On December 12, 1894, he was convicted of murder, later to be sentenced to life in prison. Before pronouncing his sentence, Judge Stevens asked Kelley if he had anything to say, to which he replied, "This whole thing is a job of Detective Welch and Larry Sullivan. I had nothing whatever to do with killing George W. Sayers."

While Bunco lay languishing in the jailhouse, Jim Turk died at his son Charles's place in Tacoma. With Jim Turk gone, Frank Turk and Paddy Lynch had grandiose ideas of becoming a big Pacific Coast concern, which would be laughable to Sullivan were it not such a belligerent affront. Sullivan now had some very powerful friends, men in high places who needed his money. Turk and Lynch would find that their way in the world was about to become more difficult than they had ever imagined.

Oregon State Penitentiary cabinet card–style mugshot of Joe "Bunco" Kelley. *Oregon State Archives, 3364.*

With powerful friends and money, Larry Sullivan began to think of himself as invincible, especially when his blood alcohol level was elevated. This brought him unneeded trouble but trouble that somehow still managed to evaporate as if by magic. One evening in May 1895, while drinking in the famous North End Tivoli Theater Saloon, Sullivan became enraged at U.S. district attorney Murphy, beating him black and blue. When the badly injured Murphy did not show up to testify at the police court trial, Sullivan was set free without bond. He immediately set out for a nearby saloon, where he preceded to drink himself drunk. Stepping from the saloon, he grabbed a passing gentleman, a banker of the San Francisco and London Bank named Quinton Macphall, and beat him terribly—until he was pulled off by his friends. During the same week, he was fined ten dollars in East Portland for delivering a beating to Paddy Lynch, the only one of the three who had it coming. When Sullivan was tried for his assault on Quinton Macphall, he was fined a mere twenty dollars, the same fine as a man was given that day by the same judge for dumping stable refuse. Getting a name for beating up innocent people would have probably not been the best business plan had Sullivan been in a business where brawn was less important than brains. Even so, I imagine the soft-spoken Peter Grant had some long talks with Sullivan about his public image.

VOTING, NORTH END STYLE

The Grant brothers had political leanings, as did Larry Sullivan, who, along with Jack Grant, became a member of the Acme Republican Club of Portland.[99] The hours they spent socializing with the Republican "machine" allowed them to see how things worked behind the scenes, and once they laid eyes on the gleaming controls of this splendid engine, they were no longer content to be mere bystanders. By the time of the 1896 Republican primaries, Larry Sullivan was the Republican Party ward captain for the North End, or Ward 2, whereas Peter Grant oversaw the voting in Ward 3.

Using their underworld connections, Sullivan and Grant hatched a scheme for the 1896 Republican senatorial primaries that would make them two very important cogs in the machine of power and would assure that their man, Joseph Simon, would be elected over George Williams, the grand old favorite of the GOP. In this scheme, not only would they supply money for Simon's campaign, but they would also guarantee him votes, placed by flesh-and-blood voters. They incorporated the assistance of two notorious criminals, Sandy Olds and George D. Barrett, to pull off a "colonization of voters" scheme. The scheme was far from secret (although one would not hear a whisper of it in the staunchly Republican *Oregonian*). A reporter for a Salem newspaper reported, "A noticeable thing is the presence of a large number of strange men in the city, who it is charged have been brought here for the sole purpose of voting, early and often."[100]

Before election day, Olds and Barrett had been bringing all manner of hoboes and itinerate workers into town to do the civic duty of voting—which, of course, was utterly illegal, immoral and foolhardy. The men were given train tickets to Portland, where they were set up in flophouse hotels. Olds and Barrett went so far as to prop up a special "rescue mission" at Third and A Streets that was given the name "Friends of the Homeless"[101] and was filled to overflowing with illegal voters.

When election day came, the polling place for Ward 2 was in the dining room of the Sailor's Home on Second Street, but the new "colonizers" were voting all over the city, moving from polling place to polling place. Not only were the "colonizers" there to "vote early and often," but they were also instructed to keep as many honest citizens from voting as possible. In the distribution of duties, Simon's men were in charge of polling, and Williams's men were in charge of the police.

At about two o'clock in the afternoon, the police were directed to go and arrest Larry Sullivan for interfering with the voting. Sullivan, surrounded by some runners he used for "muscle," grabbed a shotgun and retreated to a second-floor window, from which he declared he would kill the first man who attempted to arrest him or who tried to take the ballot box. When the day was done, Simon appeared to have won, but since the opposition was not to be bullied, the election was challenged and went through two sessions of the legislature before it was decided.

The 1896 primary may not have been Sullivan's first attempt at "colonization of voters," and it wasn't the last—although had Sullivan paid his bills, a caper he pulled in 1898 might have gone unnoticed. Two months after the election, the owner of the Washington Hotel around the corner from Sullivan's place took Sullivan to court to collect the money due for housing eighty-six men the night before the election.[102]

THE PORTLAND CLUB

At the end of the nineteenth century, there were two main categories of politicians in Portland: those who decried vice and those who made money from vice. The Chinese lotteries, faro games, poker rooms and casinos scattered across the city and concentrated in the North End made a lot of money for a sizeable number of gentlemen whose buttocks graced the pews around town on a Sunday morning. Some of the holders of high public office were not averse to leasing properties to be used as brothels. Officers designated as "special policemen" were paid one dollar per month salary by the city while collecting regular fines from gambling dens and houses of prostitution. The moneys accrued by these fines were substantial and were most certainly intended somehow for the city coffers, but the details on this sort of information are not easy to come by. The arrangement was not entirely secret. It was described by Oregon patriarch and one-time mayor of

Fifth Street looking toward the Portland Club, the two-story building on the left. *City of Portland archives, A2005-001.900.*

Portland George Williams as a necessary evil. In an article in *Pacific Monthly* magazine, contributed to by Mayor Williams, the system is described in these terms: "No binding compact has been made between the Mayor or the police and the gamblers of Portland, nor are the gamblers licensed—the method adopted, instead of a number of irregular raids and irregular fines, being a regular monthly raid and a regular monthly fine."[103]

During the widest of the wide-open period in 1899, Larry Sullivan, Peter Grant, a prospecting enthusiast from Baker City named Harvey Dale and Nathan Solomon, son of a prominent milliner, pooled their resources to start Portland's classiest gambling den—a full-fledged casino, with a cigar humidor room, bar and billiards hall. It started out at 106½ Fourth Street but soon moved to an even more prestigious downtown address, 130 Fifth, between Washington and Alder, taking up the entire second floor of the building. Although the monthly dues were a mere fifty cents, the club soon had some of the most influential and wealthy Portlanders on its membership rolls.

The "puppet" mayor Williams is shown with portraits of Harvey Dale, Jack Grant, Peter Grant and Larry Sullivan on his wall in a cartoon from the *Oregon Evening Journal* (May 28, 1905).

The Portland Club is an example of one of the ways Larry Sullivan and Peter Grant diversified their income sources. Although Sullivan gave up his ownership in the club, probably for political reasons, he owned several North End saloons, including a dance hall.

Throughout this period of diversification, the crimps still worked hard at "shipping sailors." Not only was it a steady and reliable source of

"A Quintet of Boarding Masters." *From left to right*: Dick McCarron, Peter Grant, a man believed to be company clerk George Gregson, Jack Grant (seated, left) and Larry Sullivan (seated, right). *San Francisco Call* (May 5, 1899).

wealth for them, but on some perverse level, they must have also enjoyed cowing men with weaker dispositions. Since Portland was their oyster (so to speak), they must also have enjoyed the game of driving other crimps out of the business. With the sort of monopoly they were putting in place, in a seaport far from other ports, as the twentieth century approached, they discovered that absolutely outrageous blood money charges would usually be paid without much complaint. They intended to milk the blood money cow for all it was worth. Steam-powered cargo ships were on the rise, the Panama Canal was being actively planned and seamen's unions were becoming stronger: the blood money lark was bound to fail any day soon.

HOTEL FOR SAILORS AND FARMERS

During the end of the century, one of the few eyewitness reports of the Sailor's Home on Second Street was written by an itinerant worker named Hayes Perkins. As he was passing through Portland in 1898, he was waylaid by one of the Grant brothers on a North End street. Becoming a sailor seemed like a fair proposition to the young Mr. Perkins, so he returned with Mr. Grant to the Sailor's Home. In later years, he wrote in some detail of his experience there and of being "shipped." These sorts of reports are rare, mainly because people using such places were mostly illiterate. Many could only scrawl their names. Hayes describes well his introduction to the Sailor's Home but is confused about the names of Peter Grant and Dick McCarron:

> *There is a tough gang who runs this dump at Second and Glisan Streets. It has a sign bearing the legend "Hotel, For Sailors and Farmers." I suppose they make seamen out of the latter, and I am counted one of these. But I have been about boats much of my life, and have an idea it is not so good. Larry Sullivan, Dick and Jack Grant, and Pat McCarren run this place. Sullivan is head man and a surly brute and a bum prize fighter who bullies the men in this institution cruelly. The Grants are not so bad, and McCarren is best of all. There are a lot of sailors here, every man of them with a tremendous thirst and no way of satisfying it. But I've got to go now and see what I can get in the way of a sea outfit, then sign on at the British consulate, the ship being British...*
>
> *A sailor was begging Sullivan for a dollar as I left the house. "Here!" he said, handing the man ten cents. "Don't make a beast of yourself!" If others were more importunate, he slugged them, knocking them cold. No less authority than Jim Corbett, ex-heavyweight champion, says that if Sullivan would train he might easily be middleweight champion of the world. He has plenty of practice knocking these anemic sailors round. With infinite cursing and blasphemy he hurried us on board, the ship lying over at Albina.*[104]

The wording of the sign "Hotel, For Sailors and Farmers" is an interesting detail. I would imagine that in the latter nineteenth century, there was a misconception that any poor fool could go out to Oregon and homestead. The reality was that all the good land was taken during the first few years of the wagon trains. Untold hundreds of men must have come to Portland intending to settle down and start a farm, only to find themselves in a new occupation, plowing the troughs of the deep blue sea.

MYSTERIOUS BILLY SMITH AND THE WHITE BROTHERS

There was always some irrational, overgrown boy who thought that he, too, could become a shanghaier, just as today so many disenfranchised young men see the money being made by the neighborhood gangster and think that they have what it takes to enter that line of work. More often than not, it isn't wickedness or brawn that makes for a success in the underworld. These businesses are built on connections that have been made at opportune moments over time—some have these connections, others do not.

So it was when, at the end of the century, Mysterious Billy Smith came to town. He was a boxer; in fact, he is listed in the Boxing Hall of Fame as the "Dirtiest Fighter Who Ever Lived." Born Amos Smith in Nova Scotia in 1871, he fought his way up to becoming the welterweight champion of the world in 1892. There has been a good deal of speculation on why he was "mysterious," but the best reason I have heard is that "you didn't know what hit you."

By the time Smith came to Portland, his career was in decline, and after years of

high living and being cheated by promoters, he was broke. No doubt he was introduced to Larry Sullivan, Portland's pugilistic crimp, in whom he saw a mediocre boxer who was rolling in money and who was respected by politicians. Could not the "Mysterious One" do the same?

He made the acquaintance of Harry and Jim White, brothers and thugs who, at the time, worked for the Sullivan's Sailor's Home. It seems that both Smith and the White brothers figured that the name "Mysterious Billy Smith" carried enough weight to present a challenge to Sullivan—but just to be safe, they decided to operate in Albina, on the east side of the river. In those days, lower

Promotional photograph of "Mysterious" Billy Smith. *Author's collection.*

Albina was a long line of export grain warehouses ending with the Portland Flouring Mill down by Swan Island. What these three gentlemen failed to realize was the value of all the political connections Sullivan had made in recent years. In March 1902,[105] they opened their boardinghouse in Albina, a move that started a war with the White brothers' former employer.

A long series of political events involving pressure from the consular officials of Great Britain, France, Sweden, Germany and Spain had brought in stricter legislation on sailors' boardinghouses at the state level in Oregon. In February 1903, the legislature passed a bill creating the Oregon Sailor's Boardinghouse Commission to license and regulate the business of crimping. In the great wisdom of this commission, it seemed that the Portland maritime trade's interests would be best served by a sailors' boardinghouse monopoly in the hands of Sullivan and Grant Bros.[106] The Albina house operated by the White brothers and the famous pugilist Smith was denied a license and told to cease operations. The Albina crimps were outraged. They defiantly continued to operate without a license. The injustice seemed so obvious that they were able to obtain the pro bono services of an attorney who proceeded to bring a lawsuit against the members of the Oregon Sailor's Boardinghouse Commission.

Had they been good boys, had they not been known to be "quarrelsome and fighting, bullying and terrorizing seamen" (the grounds on which their license was denied),[107] they might have had a chance. As it was, continuing operations meant carrying on the same way they had before, only this time under the scrutiny of both law enforcement and Sullivan's runners. One rather large setback for the firm came in February of that year as the firm was implicated in kidnapping a sailor. The story broke with the sensational headline "Dazed with Drugs" in an item telling how the kidnapped sailor, Charles Buren, had been drugged and taken by streetcar to Vancouver, Washington, to be kept quiet about an impending investigation. The outcome of the trials that followed were that Harry White and Billy Smith were fined for harboring a seaman, but James White was sentenced to one year in the penitentiary.[108] This ended James's career as a crimp, with him having no more stomach for the business afterward.

With his brother in the penitentiary and "Mysterious" Billy having his marriage ending in a serial soap opera followed by thousands of newspaper readers, Harry White went across the river to the old sailors' hotel on Second Street to beg for his job back. Sullivan, who was too busy in politics to spend time shipping sailors, was happy to hire him to give Jack Grant a hand shipping sailors.

After the crimping business failed, Smith found himself being beaten in the ring and beaten in the divorce court by his young (she was fourteen when she married him) wife. "Mysterious" Billy also went to Sullivan, hat in hand, and came away managing Sullivan's saloon on Third Street, the Atlantic Café. To his credit, Sullivan did not bear grudges. Billy had beaten him severely in a fight a couple of years earlier—but then pugilists are raised not to hold grudges against those with whom they make battle.

As Well Known in London as King George

Sullivan had ambition that reached beyond cowing sailors and shipping landlubbers. In March 1904, he sold his interest in the Portland Club to Nate Solomon, and one month later, he announced his retirement from the sailors' boardinghouse business. He was already famous around the world. When introduced to one ship's captain, the man said, "You're as well known in London as King George the Fifth!"[109] The era was coming to an end, and Sullivan was not going to be taken down with it.

Chapter 13

RED LIGHTS BURN OUT IN THE NORTH END

WIDE OPEN NO MORE

Being a citizen of Whitechapel, like being from Slabtown or Goose Hollow or Sullivan's Gulch, gave a poor person in Portland a sense of identity, even community. When the citizens of Whitechapel, otherwise known as Portland's Ward 2 on the political map, were asked for nominations to the city council seat for their ward, Larry Sullivan got the highest number of votes. He made it no secret that he had political ambitions, and he could stump with the populist sort of simple, straight talk and enthusiasm that Americans loved. When campaigning for the seat, he told reporters that the school kids needed schoolbooks, and if the city couldn't buy them, he would buy them for every school kid in his ward with his own money[110]—a safe sort of offer in a ward filled with single men and prostitutes. When election day was over, Larry lost by just a handful of votes. Good old "wide open Williams" was not to become mayor again, either—the vote having gone to an anti-vice reformer named Harry Lane.

Reformers were coming out of the woodwork in Portland in those days. A year earlier had seen the election of Tom Word, a prohibition Democrat and anti-vice zealot, as sheriff. He was the sort of man who was known to have jumped out of his carriage on Third Street just because he caught a whiff of opium smoke and traced it to its source and arrested several stunned inhabitants of a hithertofore unharassed den. A few months after Larry Sullivan sold his share of the Portland Club to Nate Solomon, Sheriff Tom

Tom Word election card. *Author's collection.*

Word showed up with a posse of heelers to carry off all the slot machines and roulette wheels. This was while the club was getting heat from all over the place for having been caught using marked decks. It was estimated that, using this method, the club made $20,000 in profits in one month.[111]

That evening, the headlines in the *Oregon Journal* read "Wide Open No More."[112] Word and his men had shut down not only the Portland Club but also all the other notorious dens in the city, from poker at Erickson's to fan-tan games in Chinatown. Sheriff Word would see that shutting down vice was not an easy operation in Portland, but the tide was now turning and would continue to turn in favor of reform until all the red lights above the cribs were extinguished, all the saloons were serving soda pop and the gambling dens were boarded up homes for rodents and bats.

By August 1905, Larry Sullivan was out of work, having lost the election he had planned to win. If a report in the *Oregon Journal* is to be believed, the last straw for him remaining in Portland was a scheme he cooked up with E.B. Colwell, chairman of the Republican central committee, to monopolize garbage service in the city—a lark that made gangsters rich on the East Coast. When rumors spread that this was in the works, the outcry against it was strong, and the scheme vanished.[113]

Since most of Sullivan's money had been tied up in vice of some sort, Tom Word had cost him a lot of money. When September came, Sullivan took his last $1,400 out of the bank and, along with Pete Grant, bought a train ticket for Goldfield, Nevada. Where the idea came from is not known, but it may have come from Harvey Dale, the former partner in the Portland Club, a man who was familiar with the mining industry.

JACK GRANT AND "SHANGHAI" WHITE

When, after a visit to Portland, Larry and Pete returned to Goldfield, they took Jack Grant along to help referee what came to be called the "Longest Fight" between Joe Gans and Jack Nelson. This fight is famous among boxing history enthusiasts and can even be seen online today as it was recorded on film by the Edison Company, a copy of which lies in the online archives of the Library of Congress.

Following the fight, Jack returned to the hotel for sailors on Second Street, where he continued to "ship sailors" with Harry White under the new guidelines of the state of Oregon. These guidelines limited the amount that a boardinghouse could charge as fees and did away with any sort of advanced wages or money being handed back to captains. In 1912, Jack was even made the Oregon state shipping commissioner. He was always well liked, a sportsman in demand up and down the Pacific Coast as a boxing referee. As his old boss was constantly in the news for assault, Jack was constantly in the news for his skills as a referee. It can't be said for certain whether there was any shanghaiing going on at the Sailor's Home by the Steel Bridge, but the evidence seems to be all to the contrary.

On into the twentieth century, Harry White loved to pretend that he was some kind of underworld character, adopting the name "Shanghai" White as his own. I have met people who tell me their grandfathers were "shanghaied" by "Shanghai" White. When I pin them down on a period of time, it is usually the early 1920s. This is due to the fact that sailors who shipped using a sailors' boardinghouse would nearly always refer to it as being "shanghaied," even if they were in full cooperation with the effort. It was far more colorful to tell the grandkids that you were shanghaied than to say that you met with a shipping master and signed articles.

THE LAST BOYS WHO WOULD BE CRIMPS

In 1900, Charles Jost, a lanky farm boy from the dry land wheat fields of Gilliam County, was thrust into the spotlight by winning the welterweight title for Oregon. After spending the next seven years winning and losing matches around the Pacific Coast, it became obvious to the young man that he would never make any real money as a pugilist. It seems he followed much the same logic as "Mysterious" Billy Smith toward a decision to make a career change. In fact, one of his associates spurring on his decision was the very same "Mysterious" Billy.

In July 1907, Joe "Bunco" Kelley was pardoned by the governor and returned to Portland a free man after spending thirteen years in the Gothic hell in Salem known as the "state pen." After a period of walking around feeling, in his words, "like Rip Van Wrinkle," he needed to start earning some money to help him print the prison memoirs he was sure the world was anxious to buy.[114] The trouble with this plan was that—even though he thought of himself as a world famous shanghaier—he was a mere thug from Portland, and even Portland had forgotten him.

He could still draw a small crowd to a North End saloon table, eager to hear the bunk from the very mouth of Bunco Kelley. It is not known how many of the outlandish stories that Stewart Holbrook told of Bunco Kelley were ones Kelley had invented for himself, but after being let out of prison at age sixty-one, broken in spirit and broke, stories were all he had left.

If I had to guess, I would say that it was during the late autumn of that year, at Erickson's Saloon, that Charles Jost, his brother and his fellow pugilist "Mysterious" Billy met Bunco Kelley. I chose Erickson's because "Jumbo" Riley was involved—the famous ex-pugilist, barkeep and bouncer of that same establishment. After a period of lubrication, the topic turned to the inadequacy of the establishment being run by White and Grant to meet the demand of the port. How hard could it be, they wondered, to take on a couple of smoothies like Harry White and Jack Grant? The plan was talked about through many nights of boozing. According to Bunco, they didn't need a boardinghouse, just some place to keep the sailors quiet until shipping time. If they didn't have a boardinghouse, why would they need a license? The new effort was to be conducted under the name of the Jost Brothers, since that name was as yet unsullied by association with criminal actions.

During January 1908, Bunco Kelley combed the saloons, as he had done in the days of yore, looking for jack-tar. "Mysterious" Billy was at it as well, avoiding any chance of meeting Harry White or Jack

Erickson's Cafe and Concert Hall, home of many a successful recruiting of crew members. *City of Portland archives, A2004-001.230.*

Grant. Even old three-hundred-pound "Jumbo" Riley was soliciting for the boys over whiskeys. Then it was curtains—the Jost Brothers were arrested for conducting a sailors' boardinghouse business without a license. Furthermore, they were told they would never get a license if they associated with the likes of Bunco Kelley or "Mysterious" Billy. The freight differential levied against Portland because of difficulties related to crimps had just been removed. Those involved in the maritime trade were not going to allow the old ways to be reinstated by a couple of punch-drunk kids, an obese bouncer and a withered old crimp.

After the smoke settled, the brothers tried to go through the proper channels to obtain a license. They were denied, tainted by association with bad people from the bad old days. By this time, "Mysterious" Billy was up to his neck with troubles of his own, and Bunco Kelley was touring the Northwest trying to sell his prison memoirs, *Thirteen Years in the Oregon State Penitentiary*. While he was away in prison, Portland had tripled in size. Few people even knew who this broken old man with a box of self-published books was, and of the ones who did, few cared enough to buy his book. Before long he was gone, the rumor around Erickson's being that he went to California.

THE RED LIGHTS BURN OUT

After Tom Word wiped out gambling in Portland, it soon came back like dandelions on the lawn. It would take years to nearly eradicate it, and then it would only return sanctioned by the state lottery and the Indian casinos. Open prostitution was a different matter. For years, the "wide open" policy that reigned in the city meant a North End that rivaled any of the wanton districts in the history of man. Some of the houses of prostitution were hastily built sheds with "cribs," like stalls in a stable. Others were in elegant homes with women from as far away as Paris or Berlin. Some of the saloons, like Erickson's, had an upstairs bawdyhouse with small rooms lining a long hallway. The women harassed men in the streets and solicited customers from the windows of their rooms.

Mayor Harry Lane did not subscribe to the notion that the city was best served by a system of regular fines levied on places where illicit activities were carried out. He was elected as a reformer, and reform he must. He set the night of October 5, 1908, as the date the red lights would go out in Whitechapel. Any prostitute remaining would be arrested. The "notorious houses" of downtown would be searched for refugees. When nightfall came, many of the places had been emptied out, but with the scores of women who remained, there was sense of desperation. This was the end.[115]

The city would pay train fare and expenses for any prostitute to move to any other city in America. There were rooms available in hotels for women who wanted to submit to the city's plan for dealing with them. An unnamed

Right: Harry Lane, reformer mayor of Portland and U.S. senator. *Harris & Ewing collection, Library of Congress, LC-H261- 2290.*

Below: John Clark, reformer police chief, 1913–17. Photographer unknown. *Author's collection.*

group of reformers were providing this escape. Should a woman wish to change her vocation, there were groups of reformers willing to assist in any way possible. The rest of the women, the ones who just wanted to stay and work their trade, would be arrested. This night changed the district called "Whitechapel," or the "Bad Lands," forever. There would continue to be prostitution in the city, but the "red light district" would never return to the North End.

The saloons would continue on until the reform movement, the women's suffrage movement and Governor Oswald West would work together to see the state go dry on January 1, 1916—four years earlier than the rest of the nation. By the time America entered World War I in 1917, the Wild West was dead. The palmy days of Jim Turk, Larry Sullivan and Bunco Kelley, like a bad dream, were forgotten in the progressive rush and tussle of a new century.

Chapter 14

THE UNQUIET GRAVES

A cold wind lifts the willow wisps,
Above the unquiet graves,
Beyond the harbor, filled with ships,
A tempest heaves the waves.
—Anonymous

TURKS

The funeral of James Turk was held at Holman's Undertaking Parlor at 2:00 p.m. on January 7, 1895. He was then taken by horse-drawn hearse across the Willamette to the Lone Fir Cemetery and laid to rest between his beloved wife, Catherine, and his mother. The pallbearers were Jack Grant, Larry Sullivan, Paddy Lynch, Dick McCarron, Frank Turk and George Powers.[116] The service was officiated by Reverend George Rasmus of Grace Episcopal Church. No eulogy was given. The inscription on his tombstone simply reads: "Father."

Records show that Charles Turk returned to Tacoma and worked as a hotel clerk.[117] By 1899, Charles was in the Multnomah County Poor Farm (now McMenamin's Edgefield Inn). His fortune would change with World War I; like Larry Sullivan, he would find work in the shipyards.

Frank, driven out of Portland by Sullivan and company, took his new wife, Estrella, to Honolulu, Hawaii, where he introduced Portland-style crimping. He had much sorrow with the police and other crimps, and his activities

Lone Fir Cemetery, resting place of Jim and Kate Turk. *From* The West Shore *(1888).*

provided much entertaining reading to the readers of island newspapers. Once, in 1902, when Frank was incarcerated for thirty days, his feisty Estrella walked down to the sailors' boardinghouse and began running things like a "boss shanghaier." The *Hawaiian Sun* toasted her success.[118]

The stormy marriage came to a dramatic end when during an argument, the abusive Frank Turk made as though (according to Estrella's testimony) he would cause her bodily harm with a gun. She then fired off four shots with her own "small gun," one of them lodging in her husband's leg. The story was reported in the *Honolulu Evening Bulletin* under the heading "Turks on the Warpath."[119] Much to his wife's chagrin, Frank was not seriously injured. After the divorce, Frank worked for a while on Oahu as a prison guard. Records then show that he returned to the mainland and worked for many years as a hotel runner and hotel bus driver in San Francisco. He died in that city the first day of November 1940.[120]

SULLIVAN

Larry Sullivan became wealthy nearly overnight after moving to Goldfield, Nevada. There he opened a gambling saloon called the Palace. He visited Portland less than a year later, wearing a watch chain made from gold nuggets and bringing with him a gold bar worth $60,000 to show off to his friends.[121] While working in his casino, he met a freelance newspaper writer and bunco man named George Graham Rice. Together, they started the L.M. Sullivan Trust Company, supposedly a mining investment firm. The company included Pete and Jack Grant among its members. The main efforts of the firm were to place full-page ads in dozens of national papers, from the *San Francisco Call* to the *New York Times*, advertising itself as a solid investment. Rice was skilled at spinning a good story to the business sections of papers as well. The L.M. Sullivan Trust was a Ponzi scheme that built assets to about $8 million before crashing into nothing during the panic of 1907. For a while, Sullivan was rubbing shoulders with banker millionaires. Nevada governor John Sparks, director of Bullfrog Rush Mining Company, endorsed his advertisements with his name. There was talk of making Sullivan a senator from Nevada. At the very height of his wealth and power, he co-promoted with millionaire promoter Tex Rickard one of the most famous boxing matches of all time, held at Goldfield, Nevada: the Joe Gans versus "Battling" Nelson match of 1907.[122]

After Mabel, his first wife, divorced him, taking the children, Sullivan chased the mining mirage to Mexico, landing a job as manager of the Santa Cruz mine, ninety-six miles inland from the port of Mazatlán.[123] When the mine turned out to have no metal (precious or otherwise), Sullivan abandoned the dream of becoming a mining tycoon. He was spent down to his last copper.

Through one of his many connections, he landed a job with Los Angeles attorney Clarence Darrow, who was working as the defense for the McNamara brothers, arrested for bombings arising from labor union strife. The McNamaras had blown up the *Los Angeles Times* building, killing twenty-one and injuring over one hundred people. Sullivan was on the payroll as a detective, a skill set he was not known to possess. After the trial, in which the brothers pled guilty, Sullivan was among those questioned before a grand jury investigating jury bribing during the trial. That was a skill Sullivan did possess—however, he was not charged with a crime in this case.[124]

In the spring of 1914, Sullivan was in the news for trying to swindle Mrs. Laura L. Rodgers, a wealthy divorcee, who had sued her ex-husband two years earlier for divorce on account of cruelty. Sullivan had been wooing Mrs. Rodgers and then suddenly disappeared with several thousand dollars. Chief Los Angeles County detective Samuel Browne encouraged Mrs. Rodgers to bring charges against Sullivan. At this point, Sullivan returned suddenly and, meeting Browne on the street, proceeded to beat him to a pulp (so to speak). Sullivan then promptly asked Mrs. Rodgers to be his bride, charges were dropped and wedding bells were announced.[125] It was a wedding Sullivan then managed to avoid—which was a good thing, Sullivan having married around this time a lovely bawdyhouse madam named Lucille Ayers.

To get back into the game of moneymaking, Sullivan then went to work for the Hermosillo and Nacional lotteries, which operated rather openly in Southern California. When the clamps came down on this racket in May 1915, Sullivan at first represented himself to lottery officials as being connected to the U.S attorney's office and then attempted to bribe his way out of trouble. He was subsequently convicted of mail fraud and jailed for a short period.[126]

Lucille Ayers had been arrested in 1913 for operating a "disorderly house and blind pig" in the Willamette Heights district of Portland. It was a place with a prestigious address, 349 Twenty-eighth Street North (according to the old system). This put it at Twenty-eighth and Savier, surrounded by the Victorian elegance of the new bourgeois. Following her arrest, she managed to skip town, avoiding trial. When the liquor confiscated in the raid disappeared into the handbags and holsters of city employees, the blind pig charge had to be dropped.[127]

By the time Larry Sullivan got back to Portland in December 1916, the new Oregon prohibition against liquor was in force. Larry went into business with Martin Denny, a local character well known to the police. They purchased a former bar called the Friar's Club on the outskirts of town. The business was on the books as a café with dancing, but a more accurate description would be "blind pig." Sullivan and Denny's business relationship soon began to deteriorate until it reached a point where Sullivan told the barkeeper, William Lacy, to keep Denny off the premises. This created a bloody battle between the two men. Denny was cut badly by an ice pick wielded by Lacy, while Lacy was subjected to fists and broken glass. Once in the clink, Lacy began to unburden himself with all the unholy goings-on at the club—including liquor caches on the riverbank. The place was raided at 2:30 a.m. the following morning. When Sullivan showed up later in the day, he was arrested for maintaining a nuisance, with his bail fixed at $1,000.[128]

Sullivan was still able to call in old favors, it seems—he never spent a day in jail. In August 1917, he was convicted of various charges relating to bootlegging but was pardoned by Republican governor James Withycombe. The governor stated that Sullivan and his family had suffered enough disgrace. His pardon stipulated that he must work to pay his fine of $250. Larry Sullivan was given a job as a watchman at the Foundation Company shipyards, where men were working day and night to provide wooden-hulled steamships for the war effort in Europe.[129]

During this time, Sullivan was living in the house on Twenty-eighth and Savier with Lucille Ayers,[130] who had slipped back into town. It is apparent from news articles that some of his children were with him, at least his son Tim, now sixteen, and his twenty-four-year-old daughter, Winnie. By spring of the following year, Sullivan was too sick to work, having been diagnosed with Bright's disease. To make matters worse, Lucille Ayers-Sullivan was rearrested on the old charge of running a bawdyhouse. She was jailed for ninety days.[131]

Sullivan died at 7:00 p.m. on June 9, 1918, at St. Vincent's Hospital, a few blocks from his home. He was buried at Mount Calvary Cemetery, in the hills high above the city.[132] His gravestone reads: "Lawrence Malachi Sullivan, Father."

His daughter, Winnie, began disappearing at night for long periods, keeping it a mystery as to where she went. On a chill October midnight, four months after her father's death, she was discovered by a policeman in the darkness of Mount Calvary Cemetery, weeping at her father's grave. She was given into the custody of her brother.[133]

JACK GRANT

After his return from Goldfield, Jack Grant continued on as a shipping master in an office next to the old address on Second Street. He was a popular sportsman connected with the Rose City Club and well known for placing winning bets on horses.

In 1912, after Jack Grant had risen to the rank of Oregon state shipping commissioner, he was married to a woman named Sadie Travers. Their honeymoon home was described as a "pleasant house" on East Twentieth and Ash Streets, across the Burnside Bridge from the old Sailor's Home.[134]

The Grant family around 1902. *Courtesy of the Clatsop County Historical Society, Astoria, Oregon, photo CCHS 8665ooG.*

During prohibition in Oregon, Jack Grant ran a very discrete gambling club at Fifth and Oak called the Phoenix Club. Though the club was a gambling club with a full liquor bar, it was never raided—except one evening by bandits. The two perpetrators were captured and brought to trial. During the course of the trial, when their defense attorney, Paul C. Dormizer, brought up the notion that the establishment was filled with rich fellows who were drinking and gambling, the judge told him to be silent. When Dormizer persisted to ply witnesses with questions about gambling and drinking, the judge commented, "Counsel either is determined to violate directly the ruling of the court, or he does not know what he is doing." Dormizer was fined for contempt of court. Several belligerent jurors, men who most likely had no use for the operation of the club, voted "not guilty," hanging the jury. Dormizer then proceeded to bring charges against the judge. Among the charges laid against the judge was the comment, "Jack Grant, proprietor of the Phoenix Club has for 20 years been a strong influence in local politics and has conducted gambling places with impunity." The charge against the judge went nowhere, and in a new trial the bandits were found guilty.[135]

Jack Grant continued to referee boxing matches all over the Pacific Northwest, becoming one of the central figures in that sport. His name, in conjunction with boxing, was often seen in the sports pages, to the point that his connection with the maritime trade was of little interest to anyone, if at all. Those were the days when boxing was considered the sport of all sports, and Jack Grant's connection to it made him a local hero. He was described in the *Oregonian* as "one of the most efficient and popular experts in the West."[136]

In 1921, in what seemed like a replay of old practices, he was sued by the Swedish vice-consul for charging too much in supplying seamen.[137] He was still working with Harry "Shanghai" White, next door to the old sailor's home, when he died on June 23, 1921, at St. Mary's Hospital in Astoria. He had been visiting relatives when he succumbed to a heart attack. He was sixty years old. The next Friday night, at a prizefight in Portland between Willie St. Clair and Bobby Harper, the fans stood bareheaded for a moment of silence in respect for the well-loved sportsman.

The sailor's home was torn down in August 1921. The *Oregonian* commented, "What tales could be spun of this old place!" His longtime partner, Harry White, ended his days as a deputy Multnomah County sheriff, working at the new prison at Rocky Butte.

PETER GRANT

The vendetta against gambling that brought down the Portland Club left Peter Grant a near pauper. According to family oral history (told to the author by Peter Grant III), Peter's mother, Bridget, loaned him the money to follow Larry Sullivan to Nevada, where he joined in operations of the Palace Saloon, which included a hotel and casino. He was also made treasurer[138] of the L.M. Sullivan Trust. Both Peter and Jack were involved in the promotion of the Gans-Nelson prizefight. When the L.M. Sullivan Trust went into freefall, Peter disengaged himself and returned home broke again, much to his mother's dismay.

Peter then became part owner of a packing company in Astoria, most likely with a loan from his mother. During the next few years, he worked for the Rose City Club lining up pro boxing matches and, like his brother, became a well-known sportsman. In 1918, Peter secured the patent rights to a process for making paper cups, and a factory was set up in San Francisco.[139] After

Peter Grant with his great-grandson and namesake. The photo is thought by Peter Grant III to have been taken on November 1, 1947, in Pleasant Hill, California, on Peter Grant's eighty-fifth birthday. *Used by permission of Peter Grant III.*

Jack's death he moved to New York,[140] but then settled in San Francisco. He lived in San Francisco the remainder of his days, but he said, "I still think of Portland as home."[141] He died in San Francisco in 1950 at age eighty-seven. The legacy of his name, his humor and his good looks have been carried on by a grandson and great-grandson of the same name.

MRS. GRANT SUCCUMBS

Bridget Grant stopped shipping sailors around the turn of the century. She had made a pile of money, most of which was spent buying land. She was able to spend many years as a retired grande dame in the Dezendorf apartments in downtown Portland. She delighted in helping her grandchildren achieve the education that she did not have. She sent Peter's son, Richard, to Stanford, where he was a track star for the college.

It is remarkable that a poor, illiterate Irish woman, a widow with many children, was able to amass a fortune in those days. She died on December 28, 1923, at the age of eighty-eight and was put to rest next to her long-dead husband in the St. Mary's Cemetery across Stark Street from the Lone Fir Cemetery.[142] In the 1930s, the graves were dug up to make room for Central Catholic High School and moved to Mount Calvary in the West Hills. The stones were lost, so her grave, and those of her family buried there, are unmarked.

Kelley

After his failed attempts to make a living selling his book, Joe "Bunco" Kelley disappeared from sight. He may have found work with Abe Ruef, a San Francisco gangster. In November 1908, it was reported that an "undesirable" named "Bunco" Kelley worked for him as a flunky.[143] This may have been some other Kelley, given the same *nom de guerre* for having a similar proclivity toward telling tall tales. After a "book tour" of Seattle in 1909, Bunco was never heard from again. It would have amused him to have known that one hundred years after his death, he would finally become the "boss shanghaier of the Northwest," thanks to the writer Stewart Holbrook.

Lynch

After Paddy "the Canary" Lynch was released from the penitentiary in 1906, he was never able to get his foot in the crimping game but was often in trouble with the law for petty crimes and bootlegging. He lived until July 1941 and was seventy-eight when he died. He was put to rest at Mount Calvary. Bunco Kelley said that he was "called the 'Canary Bird' the first time he came to prison for swiping a canary out of a lodging house."[144]

"MYSTERIOUS" BILLY SMITH

"Mysterious" Billy Smith went through a period of tribulation arising from a messy divorce.[145] In December 1911, he nearly died after he was shot down in a gun battle with his ex-wife's husband, Captain Albert Loomis.[146] He later purchased a beer tavern in upper Albina that he named the Champion's Rest. He was a Portland fixture, refereeing boxing matches and racing horses until his death in 1937. He was laid to rest in the Pioneer Cemetery at Southeast Eighty-second and Holgate. Today, the grave has lost its marker and is just a patch of rough sod. After his death, his tavern came to be called "Mysterious Billy Smith's Tavern" until it was torn down around 1958 to make room for an expressway.

MY APOLOGY

In this book, I have brought together facts, vignettes, opinions and images out of a large variety of archives to build what I hope is a realistic picture of the shanghaiers of Oregon. None of them may have been what they appeared to others to be. Larry Sullivan may have seemed to be a greedy buffoon to many, but he had some inner quality, as a father, that brought his young daughter to weep at his grave, night after night. Jim Turk was said to have been a fair dealer who paid his debts. The love he had for his children is apparent in their desire to be like him. Some of these shanghaiers are fairly well known locally as caricatures, drawn from the writings of Holbrook. Some of them, famous in their time, are forgotten men lying in unmarked graves. Any one of them deserves, at least, his own book, chronicling his passage through a most unique and incredible time in the history of the Pacific Northwest. I advise anyone who joins me in the task of bringing these historical figures into the light to avoid all fictions and stick fast to the truth, which, in the case of these individuals, is stranger and far more satisfying than fiction.

A TALL TALE OF TUNNELS

ORIGINS OF THE TALE

Each city, town and neighborhood has its "urban legends" and lore of dubious authenticity. The origins of most of these tales are unknown, but in the case of the legend of Portland's "shanghai tunnels"—one of the most prevalent of all Portland myths—its origin can almost certainly be pinpointed to the very day it was first proclaimed to the world.

Oregonian reporter Robert Olmos started on the job in December 1962 and early in his career at the *Oregonian* started writing feature stories from Portland's skid row around lower Burnside. Doubtless he got an earful from the denizens of watering holes, retelling tales of the area's nefarious past—gambling, prostitution, dirty politics and shanghaiing. In his third month on the job, he was called to report on the demolition of a building at 1211–1215 Southwest Second in downtown Portland, where a secret passage was discovered. He identified this as being a Chinese gambling den, but in the subheading, he added the words, "Old Buildings Contained Secret Tunnels to Waiting Ships."[147] Olmos then proceeded to tell of a secret room on the second floor of the building, hidden behind a reinforced door. The room was filled with Chinese gambling paraphernalia, betraying its past. Even though this room was on the second floor, Olmos couldn't help adding, "The location also is believed to have had an underground tunnel that once led to the waterfront. Along these tunnels shanghaied sailors were carried to waiting ships."[148]

This article appeared on the front page of the *Oregonian* that day and was seen by tens of thousands of Oregonians. The tunnel story must have been fresh in Olmos's mind, having been recently concocted. It was not a story that had been in circulation for very long.

This can be shown by another *Oregonian* article a few years earlier, written by the well-known, ex-logger, "rough writer" Stewart Holbrook. Holbrook made a very good living by writing interesting, semi-historical stories. Where the facts were not colorful enough, Holbrook could add great daubs of color with ease—just as he did with the comical, semi-historical oil paintings he created under the pseudonym, "Mr. Otis."[149] His artistic efforts brought him acclaim in the New York art world,[150] and the historical "facts" he invented stole their way into history books. In July 1957, Holbrook retold one of his favorite old chestnuts for the enjoyment of the *Oregonian* audience, a story called "How the *Flying Prince* Got Its Name." In this Munchausian fable, the well-known shanghaier Bunco Kelley happens across twenty-four winos (the number changes each time the story is told) who had broken into the basement of an undertaker, thinking it was the "Snug Harbor" saloon. They had tapped open a keg of formaldehyde (thinking it was some sort of exotic booze) and proceeded to poison themselves. Seeing this ghastly display, the enterprising Bunco (who had been fruitlessly searching for sailors to crew on the *Flying Prince*) made haste to a nearby livery stables to hire men (at five dollars each) to help him load the dead and dying winos onto wagons and to haul them off to Ainsworth dock where the *Flying Prince* was moored. The next day as the *Flying Prince* headed out to sea, the poor captain found that he had a macabre crew stowed in the forecastle (the men being by that time in the throes of rigor mortis).[151]

Not only was this story believed to be a part of Portland history by some, I am sad to say it can be found without irony in some history books. I could debunk the tale line by line, but the important thing is this: had Holbrook thought there were "shanghai tunnels," he would have used them to get the winos to the dock. Holbrook had been around long enough, just like the Chinese who put their gambling den on the second floor, to know that basements and tunnels were useless near the waterfront during the yearly period of high water—October into June. The idea of a "shanghai tunnel" would have been especially laughable to those people you see in the old photos rowing boats around the lower part of the city during floods.

Holbrook has become the final word on Portland history for many, especially those interested in the shanghaiing days. In 1933, Holbrook put together a series of *Sunday Oregonian* features on Portland's nefarious history of brothels, saloons and shanghaiers. The series lasted for eight consecutive Sundays with the two-cents-worth added from every toothless skid row octogenarian who could still sit up on a bar stool. The series is filled with hearsay, half-truths and balderdash, but there is not a single mention of "shanghai tunnels." The old waterfront had given way to a seawall by then, but the old-timers still had soggy memories of the wet old days when water liked to come lapping around the upper wharves.

Here are a few more reasons the "shanghai tunnels" story is untrue.

1. Prior to around 1900, when the river was finally dredged to twenty-five feet, the river was too shallow for many oceangoing windjammers to top off at the Portland grain docks, flour mills and lumber docks, except in very high water.[152] Thus they finished loading in Astoria, with cargo being sent down by barge and steam tug. That meant the sailors signed on to vessels and joined them in Astoria. In fact, so many sailors were signed in Astoria that Portland lost its U.S. shipping commissioner (the official charged with overseeing signing sailors on American ships) to Astoria. Portland was without a U.S. shipping commissioner from about 1886 into the twentieth century.

2. Men who signed as sailors but then were unwilling to go to sea were put aboard by armed guards or special U.S. marshals. They were taken by steamboat to Astoria, where their ships would be anchored. This was to make sure their contracts were fulfilled. A sailor's contract was as binding as joining the armed services—a fact that was made evident in that sailors were exempt from the freedoms given to slaves by the Thirteenth Amendment of the U.S. Constitution.

3. If a "guest" at a sailors' boardinghouse seemed unwilling to become a sailor, the boardinghouse keeper would send a runner (or hired imposter) to either the British consul in Astoria (Peter L. Cherry) or in Portland (James Laidlaw) or to the U.S. shipping commissioner in Astoria (C.P. Upshur) to sign the names of people under their charge. Once the person's name was signed, even though the signature was forged, the law would see them on board. There was no need to use a tunnel. If the person was unwilling to go aboard, they were taken there by force or under the influence of drink or drugs.

4. The fact that ships finished loading in Portland only when the river was quite high means that if there were tunnels to the docks (which there were not), the tunnels would have been filled with water.

5. The docks close to the city were steamboat docks and boathouses. The export grain docks, flour mills and lumber docks were either in

Albina or on the west bank, north of where Alber's Mill was built in 1910—they were nowhere near the secret passages of Chinatown.

6. The secret passages in Chinatown were used exclusively by Chinese as a means of escape from fan-tan parlors, gambling rooms and opium dens in case of raids by opposing tongs or the police. In 1914, the city council tried to outlaw secret passages but was opposed by the Chinese business community as being unconstitutional and discriminating against Chinese.[153]

7. After much research, I have found no record or any mention of so-called shanghai tunnels or any other waterfront tunnels in any publication prior to the 1963 *Oregonian* article by Olmos.

THE LOADING OR UNLOADING OF VESSELS VIA TUNNELS

In the early 1970s, Portland restaurateur Gary Cooper opened a bar called Darby O'Gill's in the old town New Market Theater. In 1972, he opened an extension, Darby's Below Decks, in the restaurant basement. There was a drainage creek running through the basement to the Willamette Creek tunnel. Cooper turned this old brick viaduct into dining alcoves, calling it a "Shanghai Tunnel."[154] Old maps show ravines with streams running through what is now downtown Portland. Long ago these were put in culverts and covered over to create more real estate for houses and businesses. It was the remains of one of these tunnels that Mr. Cooper used for his basement extension. What he did about the rats is unknown.

At some point, some thoughtful souls must have wondered why someone would go to all the expense to have such an expansive tunnel built just to shanghai sailors. One answer occurred to them: it must have been originally built to load and unload ships in the rain. Whoever came up with this idea—one that prevails today—never bothered to see if such a thing had ever been done in the history of seaports, let alone the history of Portland. The tunnels being full of water for the greater part of the year, the cargo would have been submerged and ruined, just as the shanghaied victims would have been drowned. Demurrage lawsuits were common, arising from ships laying over at Portland wharves for overly long periods due to endless weeks of rain. If common sense doesn't put the "ship loading tunnels" theory to rest, the list of demurrage lawsuits should show that shippers were helpless against weeks upon end of "Oregon mist." In the text of the demurrage lawsuits, the entire loading and unloading process in Portland is examined—of course, any mention of tunnels is absent.[155]

In the exhaustively precise 1889 Sanborn Insurance maps of Portland, every visible detail—every entryway, egress, stair, inner room, clearstory, loading ramp, skylight, etc.—is noted, along with wood piles and underground cisterns for firefighting. In these maps, there is nothing resembling a tunnel anywhere on the working waterfront.

A TOURIST ATTRACTION IS BORN

The budding "shanghai tunnels" legend was taken up in the 1970s by young people wishing to conjure history from the basements of old buildings and the tall tales of anyone old enough to be on social security. The tale took on a life of its own—especially as lucrative tours were organized. Today, tours of the basement areas of "old town" are a well-publicized tourist activity. The tours include stories of thousands of shanghaied men being carried to slavery on ships with amazingly large crews. The only truth to these stories is this: yes, there were some people who were shanghaied in Portland, Oregon. However, the likelihood of any of them being shanghaied via a tunnel is nil.

A FORGOTTEN BUSINESS

From all of the reading I have done on this subject, I would surmise that it is possible there were between one to two hundred people actually shanghaied (as opposed to saying that they were "shanghaied" after being cajoled into signing ships papers) in the port cities of Astoria and Portland in the years between 1873 and 1908. The number may have been less. One authority on the subject was James Laidlaw, British vice-consul, who lived in Portland from 1875 until his death in 1913. In 1905, Laidlaw was asked by a group of young people whose friend had suddenly sailed for England if he thought their friend had been shanghaied. In an article titled, "A Forgotten Business," the *Daily Oregon Journal* published his reply.

> *"Sailors," said Mr. Laidlaw, "are rarely shanghaied now—there are not nearly so many cases as the public has been led to believe. Every sailor*

making the trip has to appear in the consul's office and sign the shipping articles in his own handwriting. Before he is asked to do so the consul reads the articles in his presence and explains what duties will be required of him. Then the applicant is asked if he is willing to do so: he does it of his own free will.

"While residing at Portland I have known of a few shanghaiing cases, but those happened in the early days. The way they did is was this: Just before her departure the sailor boarding-house people took a sailor to a ship under some pretense or other, where he was held until the vessel was ready to sail. In the meantime a confederate of the gang went to the consul's office and signed the name of the prisoner to the shipping articles. Then the vessel left for the sea and the captive's pleadings for release would be in vain. It would be shown him that his name was on the roll of those who had agreed to make the voyage and there the matter ended. That is the only manner in which a sailor can be shanghaied—it is by some one else personating [sic] *him.*

"Paddy Lynch, formerly the sailor boarding-house proprietor at Astoria is now serving a term in the state penitentiary for committing this offense. No, the shanghai evil has never flourished in Portland to any great extent."[156]

So, here we have it, the official statement on the matter. The Honorable Mr. James Laidlaw may be downplaying things a bit, seeing how the offices of the British vice-consul in Astoria and Portland were complicit in shipping of any landlubber whose name was forged in their presence. None of the boarding masters were above the actual, physical shanghaiing of innocent strangers, but with a combination of fortune-seekers and hoboes wandering through town, and strict vagrancy laws to keep them from sleeping on park benches, the need to do so would arise very rarely. When the need did arise, it is a good thing for them that there were ignorant hoodlums handy, like Paddy "the Canary" Lynch, to hang the whole thing on.

NOTES

CHAPTER I

1. *Daily Morning Astorian*, August 21, 1890.
2. *San Francisco Directory and Business Guide* (San Francisco: Towne & Bacon Printers, 1868), 535.
3. State of California, Liquor Tax Register, 1866; *San Francisco Directory and Business Guide* (San Francisco: Towne & Bacon Printers, 1867).
4. *Daily Alta California*, "Murder," November 10, 1869.
5. Ibid., "The Dutch Aleck Murder," November 12, 1869.
6. *Sacramento Daily Union*, December 2, 1870.
7. *Improvement of Lower Willamette and Columbia Rivers from Portland, Oregon, to the Sea: Oregon and Washington, Annual Reports of the War Department*, Part 3 (Washington: Government Printing Office, 1883), 2001.
8. Samuel Bowles, *Our New West* (Springfield, MA: Hartford Publishing Co., 1870).
9. *Morning Oregonian*, "Collection District of Willamette," February 8, 1870.
10. *San Francisco City Directory* (San Francisco: Edward Bosqui & Co., 1874).
11. *Daily Alta California*, "The Stolen Trunk," January 11, 1874.
12. *Morning Oregonian*, "The Turk Family," January 22, 1874.
13. *Portland City Directory* (Portland, OR: F.L. McCormick, 1875).
14. Richard Henry Dana, *The Seaman's Friend: Containing a Treatise on Practical Seamanship* (Boston, MA: Thomas Groom & Co., 1873), 216.
15. If Turk happened to be in Astoria, the approach was the same. He was a skilled boatman who often challenged others to race in Youngs Bay—sometimes even putting challenges in the *Astorian* in the form of an advertisement.
16. *Who's Who in the Northwest*, vol. 1 (Portland, OR: Western Press Association, 1911).
17. *Morning Oregonian*, September 27, 1877.
18. Ibid., September 22, 1877.

19. "The Bethel Flag," *Seaman's Friend and Naval Journal* (New York: Seaman's Friend Society, 1843), 209.
20. "Religious Interest among Sailors," *Morning Oregonian*, December 5, 1877.
21. *New Northwest*, "A Pity He Will Escape," July 3, 1879.

Chapter 2

22. *Morning Oregonian*, "Mrs. Grant Succumbs," December 18, 1923.
23. *Gloucester Directories*, 1860–1878 (Gloucester MA: Sampson, Davenport and Co.).
24. *Morning Oregonian*, July 3, 1931.

Chapter 3

25. This Jack Dempsey was the Irish-born heavyweight champion nicknamed "Nonpareil" because of his record of being unbeatable. At age thirty-two, he lost his fight with tuberculosis in Portland, Oregon, in 1895.
26. *The American Slang Dictionary* (Chicago: R. J. Kitteridge & Co., 1891). "Sand," akin to "grit," "courage."
27. *Morning Oregonian*, "Sullivan Won't Fight," October 2, 1885.
28. *Coast Mail* (Marshfield, Oregon), November 12, 1885.
29. Ibid.
30. Ibid.

Chapter 4

31. *Sunday Oregonian*, "Shanghaiing Sailors," November 17, 1901.
32. *Morning Oregonian*, September 3, 1880.
33. *Daily Astorian*, August 16, 1882.
34. "Willamette Wavelets," *Morning Oregonian*, August 28, 1882.
35. *Sacramento Record Daily Union*, March 1, 1883.
36. *Morning Oregonian*, "Shanghaied," March 7, 1883.

Chapter 5

37. "Them That Are Afar Off upon the Sea," *The Seaman's Friend*, April 1873.
38. Report of British vice consul James Laidlaw to the Marquess of Salisbury, June 29, 1898.
39. *Daily Morning Astorian*, January 15, 1885.
40. Ibid., March 19, 1885.
41. *Morning Oregonian*, "Shipping Abuses: A Seaman on Board the Clan Buchanan," June 21, 1888.

CHAPTER 6

42. *Daily Morning Astorian*, August 30, 1885.
43. Actually, the bark *Sierra Blanca*, Thompson, Anderson & Co. (Sierra Shipping), Liverpool.
44. *Morning Oregonian*, "All the Elements," September 20, 1892.
45. *Dalles Daily Chronicle*, July 18, 1891.
46. *Morning Oregonian*, "All the Elements," September 20, 1892.
47. Ibid.

CHAPTER 7

48. Ibid., "Swindled Sailors," April 19, 1893.
49. *Portland City Directory* (Portland, OR: F.L. McCormick, 1884).
50. *Willamette Farmer*, November 10, 1882.
51. *Sunday Oregonian*, October 22, 1933.
52. *Morning Oregonian*, July 26, 1884.
53. Vessels were loaded to the point where they needed to move with the tides from deep anchorage to deep anchorage in order to make it downriver. This often made for some odd hours of departure.
54. This was not the sailors' boardinghouse runner, Joseph "Bunco" Kelley. In retrospectives written in newspapers in future decades, this mistake would be made by several writers who were quick to assume and slow to research.
55. *Morning Oregonian*, "Kelley Murder," November 7, 1886.
56. Ibid., "Drugged to Death," July 9, 1886.
57. *Sunday Oregonian*, "Manslaughter," March 20, 1887.
58. *Morning Oregonian*, "Kelley Murder," November 7, 1886.
59. Ibid., "Alleged Outrageous Assault," March 22, 1887.
60. Ibid., "She Cannot Find Her Sister," April 15, 1887.
61. Ibid., "Where's Cassidy," February 21, 1885.

CHAPTER 8

62. Illegible, probably Venezuela.
63. All of the facts of this case—the ship *Xenia* in port at that time, the captain's name and the cargo—can be verified by maritime records, which support the letter as being true.
64. I am grateful to Cindy Coffin, the great-granddaughter of Carol Beeby's sister, for allowing me to print this fascinating piece of her family history.

CHAPTER 9

65. The 1900 U.S. census conducted at the Oregon State Penitentiary in Salem.
66. *Morning Oregonian*, "Will Plead His Own Case," April 22, 1887.
67. *Daily Morning Astorian*, February 11, 1887.

68. Ibid., "Can Such Things Be in Portland?" June 9, 1887.
69. *Morning Oregonian*, "A Shipmaster's Complaint," April 17, 1887.
70. *Daily Morning Astorian*, "Bunko Kelly, Shanghaier," October 29, 1890.
71. *Morning Oregonian*, "Jim Turk and Kelly," November 11, 1891.
72. Ibid., "A Samoan Survivor's Complaint," October 17, 1889.
73. Ibid., October 13, 1891.
74. Ibid., "They Were All Bound Over," November 4, 1893.

Chapter 10

75. *Sunday Oregonian*, "Before the Blind Goddess," February 17, 1889.

Chapter 11

76. *Daily Morning Astorian*, "Jim Turk and Captain Stevens," September 11, 1889.
77. Ibid., "Turks Unreasonable Appearance," September 17, 1889.
78. It is an interesting fact that throughout the many mentions of this case in the press, Jim Turk, a Portland businessman since the beginning of the 1870s, was referred to as the "Astoria Sailor's Boardinghouse keeper." The year 1889 was the only one in which Jim Turk does not appear in the *Portland Business Directory*. It is obvious he had a boardinghouse in Portland that year, since it showed up in so many police reports, but his residence was in Astoria.
79. Conjecture, of course, but his speech that night seems the speech of a sentimental drunkard.
80. In a final decision, the navy determined the rise and fall of the rivers as too unpredictable and the channel too narrow and shallow.
81. *Morning Oregonian*, "One Year's Growth," September 24, 1889.
82. Ibid.
83. *Daily Morning Astorian*, "Jim Turk Leaves Astoria Again," October 9, 1889.
84. *Morning Oregonian*, "The Turks," January 25, 1887.
85. Ibid.
86. *Daily Morning Astorian*, December 13, 1887.
87. Ibid., January 17, 1890.
88. Ibid., February 9, 1890.
89. *Morning Oregonian*, "A Combination Broken Up," January 14, 1891.
90. Ibid., "Turk and His Sailors," December 19, 1891.
91. Ibid., "Pests of the Port," December 21, 1891.
92. Ibid., "End of the Combine," January 16, 1896.
93. Ibid., "War on Gamblers," November 11, 1894.
94. Ibid., "James Turk Dead," January 5, 1895.

Chapter 12

95. Ibid., "A Master's Complaint," January 8, 1889.
96. Ibid., "Fighting over Sailors," July 31, 1892.

97. In maritime law, to detain a vessel while a lien is examined.

98. *Morning Oregonian*, "Shipping Sailors," December 9, 1892.

99. *Republican League Register: A Record of the Republican Party in the State of Oregon 1894 to 1896* (Portland, OR: Register Publishing Co., 1896).

100. *Daily Capital Journal*, April 2, 1896.

101. Ibid., May 25, 1896.

102. Ibid., August 11, 1898.

103. Charles Erskine Scott Wood, "The Suppression of Vice by Law," *Pacific Monthly* (December 1903).

104. Hayes Perkins, "Here and There: An Itinerant Worker in the Pacific Northwest, 1898," *Oregon Historical Quarterly* 102, no. 3 (Fall 2001).

105. *Morning Oregonian*, March 25, 1902.

106. Ibid., "License to Sullivan and Grant," May 27, 1903.

107. Ibid., "White and Smith Are Unfit," July 29, 1903.

108. *Morning Oregonian*, April 7, 1903.

109. Ibid., "Sullivan Well Known Here," May 22, 1915.

Chapter 13

110. *Morning Oregonian*, May 14, 1905.

111. *Daily Capital Journal*, November 26, 1909.

112. *Oregon Daily Journal*, "Wide Open No More," July 24, 1904.

113. Ibid., August 11, 1905.

114. *Morning Oregonian*, July 22, 1907

115. Ibid., "Red Lights Burn Out in North End," October 6, 1908.

Chapter 14

116. Ibid., "The Funeral of James Turk," January 8, 1895.

117. The *Tacoma City Directory* and the *Portland City Directory*.

118. *Hawaiian Sun*, "Mrs. Turk Wins Out," May 2, 1902.

119. *Honolulu Evening Bulletin*, "Turks on the Warpath," January 25, 1904.

120. Census records and Californian Death Record.

121. *Morning Oregonian*, "Mr. Lawrence M. Sullivan Greets Old Friends," November 13, 1906.

122. George Graham Rice, "My Adventures with Your Money," *Gorham Press* (Boston, MA), 1911.

123. *Los Angeles Herald*, "Flynn Takes Charge of Santa Cruz Mine," November 3, 1909.

124. *San Francisco Call*, "Mcnamara Jury Briber Sought by Officials," January 5, 1912.

125. *Daily Capital Journal*, "Wedding Will End It," March 25, 1914.

126. *Ontario Argus*, "Sullivan in Lottery Trouble," May 27, 1915.

127. *Morning Oregonian*, "Liquor Replevin Suit Off," January 5, 1916.

128. *Oregon City Courier*, "Jail for Pair," April 26, 1917.

129. *Daily Oregonian*, "Larry Sullivan at Work," August 26, 1917.

130. *Portland City Directory*, 1917.

131. *Morning Oregonian*, "Old Sentence in Force," March 26, 1918.

132. *Sunday Oregonian*, "Sullivan Is Dead," June 9, 1918.

133. Ibid., "Girl Grieves for Her Father," October 20, 1918.

134. *Morning Oregonian*, "Jack Grant Lost to Bachelors," January 13, 1912.

135. Ibid., "Court Bias Is Charged," November 13, 1918.

136. *Sunday Oregonian*, "Berg Beats Swanson," July 5, 1914.

137. *Morning Oregonian*, "Employment Agent Is Sued," August 24, 1920.

138. *San Francisco Call*, "Sullivan Company in Financial Straits," January 5, 1907.

139. *Morning Oregonian*, "Peter Grant May Leave City," July 30, 1918.

140. Ibid., July 3, 1928.

141. Ibid.

142. Ibid., "School Permit Sought," August 22, 1938.

143. *San Francisco Call*, "Abe Ruef's Gunmen Appear in Court," November 7, 1908.

144. Joseph Kelly, *Thirteen Years in the Oregon Penitentiary* (Portland, OR: self-published, 1908), 78.

145. *Morning Oregonian*, "Mysterious Billy Blames M'Carty," February 1, 1906.

146. Ibid., "Mysterious Billy Smith Shot Down," December 18, 1911.

Afterword

147. *Oregonian*, "Abandoned, Ghostly Chinese Gambling Den Found by Portland Demolition Workers," March 25, 1963.

148. Ibid.

149. *Morning Oregonian*, "Otis Lewis & Clark Due at Meir & Frank," May 12, 1959.

150. *Sunday Oregonian*, "Cause of New York Stimulating Cultural Event Familiar to Northwest Otis-Holbrook Fans," September 28, 1958.

151. *Morning Oregonian*, "How the *Flying Prince* Got Its Crew," July 7, 1957.

152. "How Deep Is My River—Part 2," Portland Waterfront History Blog, http://portlandwaterfront.blogspot.com/2013_05_01_archive.html.

153. *Morning Oregonian*, "Secret Passages May Go, Mayor Has Plan to Curb Gambling in Chinatown," September 18, 1913; "Discrimination Is Charge," March 1, 1914; "City Official Visit Mystic Chinatown—Steel Barred Doors and Secret Panels Are Inspected," February 5, 1919; and "Secret Doors under Fire," April 23, 1919.

154. *Oregonian*, "Swinging Basement," January 30, 1972.

155. See, for example, *Balfour v. Wilkins*, 5 Sawy. 429, 2 F.Cas. 539 (D. Oregon 1879) and *Kerr v. Schwaner*, 177 F. 659 (9th Cir. 1910).

156. *Morning Oregonian*, "A Forgotten Business," February 15, 1905.

INDEX

ABOUT THE AUTHOR

B arney Blalock is the author of *Portland's Lost Waterfront: Tall Ships, Steam Mills and Sailor's Boardinghouses*, published by The History Press. His love of the Portland waterfront comes from the thirty-three years he spent working on the grain docks. He is the great-grandson of Oregon pioneers and, as such, has had a lifelong interest in local history. In 2013, he delivered a series  of lectures at different Multnomah County libraries describing the facts and fiction of the old shanghaiing days. In October 2013, Barney Blalock appeared as a guest speaker on Oregon Public Television's *Oregon Experience* in a program called "Portland Noir." He is a member of the Oregon Historical Society and the Oregon Maritime Museum. In his Portland Waterfront History blog, he is able to satisfy his need to research and write on maritime subjects that are often overlooked by other Oregon history writers. He is now semi-retired and works as a writer and web manager. Father of three wonderful children and grandfather of two, Barney and his wife, Nektaria, live in Northeast Portland with their dear cat, Ralph.